GCSE English
For the Grade A*-G Resits

GCSE English and English Language are tough to master — but this brilliant CGP book covers everything you'll need to pass the exam resits in 2016 or summer 2017!

It covers the AQA, OCR and WJEC exams, with fantastic study notes explaining every topic, worked examples and plenty of all-important exam-style questions.

We've also thrown in a full set of Foundation and Higher practice papers, *and* top-notch advice for picking up marks — so you can definitely pencil yourself in for exam success.

How to access your free Online Edition

This book includes a free Online Edition to read on your PC, Mac or tablet.
You'll just need to go to **cgpbooks.co.uk/extras** and enter this code:

0503 6974 4768 0641

By the way, this code only works for one person. If somebody else has used this book before you, they might have already claimed the Online Edition.

D0318443

Complete
Revision & Practice
Everything you need to pass the exams!

Contents

Contents

Published by CGP

Editors:
Izzy Bowen
Joe Brazier
Emma Crighton

With thanks to Karen Wells for the proofreading.
With thanks to Ana Pungartnik for the copyright research.

Acknowledgements:

Fireworks and Animals leaflet on page 17 © The Blue Cross, www.bluecross.org.uk

Article entitled 'British teenager becomes youngest person to sail round the world solo' on page 18
copyright Guardian News & Media Ltd 2016

With thanks to Rex Features for permission to use the images on pages 18 and 70

Article entitled 'When Danger Starts at Home' on page 19 from Habitat for Humanity

Leaflet on page 22 from Plan UK

Article entitled 'Destination New York' on page 23 copyright Charlotte Jolly / Easy Living © The Condé Nast
Publications Ltd.

With thanks to Getty Images for permission to use the image on page 23

With thanks to iStock.com for permission to use the images on pages 23, 75 & 76

Extract from Into the Wild on page 24 by John Krakauer, Pan Macmillan, London. Copyright © John Krakauer, 1999

Article entitled 'Record Dragons' Den investment for Harry Potter-style magic wand' on page 69
© Telegraph Media Group Limited 2010

Article on page 70 © Hello! Magazine.com

Article entitled 'Piece of Isaac Newton's apple tree to experience zero gravity in space' on page 75 © The Times,
May 10th 2010 / nisyndication.com

Extract on page 77 from The Diving Bell and the Butterfly by Jean-Dominique Bauby. Reprinted by permission of
HarperCollins Publishers Ltd © 1997 Jean-Dominique Bauby

ISBN: 978 1 78294 705 9
Printed by Elanders Ltd, Newcastle upon Tyne.
Clipart from Corel®

Based on the classic CGP style created by Richard Parsons.

What You Have To Do

This book will get you prepared for your <u>GCSE English</u> or <u>GCSE English Language</u> exams if you're doing the <u>AQA</u>, <u>OCR</u> or <u>WJEC</u> specifications. Here's a quick reminder of what to expect.

There are **Higher** and **Foundation** exams

1) Whether you're taking <u>GCSE English</u> or <u>GCSE English Language</u>, the exams are exactly the <u>same</u>.

2) You could be taking <u>either</u> the <u>Higher</u> or the <u>Foundation</u> tier though — ask your teacher if you're not sure which one you're doing. The two tiers are a bit <u>different</u> — here's how:

> • The <u>Higher</u> paper covers grades <u>A*-D</u>.
> • The <u>Foundation</u> paper covers grades <u>C-G</u>.
> • In the Higher paper, the questions will usually be more <u>open-ended</u> than the ones in the Foundation paper, and you'll be asked to write more 'essay-style' answers.

3) For most exam boards there will be just <u>one exam</u>, split into Section A and Section B. If you're doing WJEC, the questions will be split into <u>two separate exams</u> — Unit 1 and Unit 2.

This book will help you to pass your exams, but check with your teacher to see what else you need to do for your resit — you might also need to redo the Controlled Assessment parts of the course.

You'll have to answer some **Reading Questions**

1) In Section A of the exam (or Unit 1 for WJEC), you'll be given some <u>non-fiction texts</u> to read. These texts are <u>unseen</u> — this means you don't get to see them before the exam.

2) You'll then have to <u>answer questions</u> about these texts — see Section 2 on pages 10-26 for more about answering reading questions.

You'll also need to do some **Writing**

1) In Section B of the exam (or Unit 2 for WJEC), you'll have to do some of your <u>own non-fiction writing</u>.

2) For <u>AQA</u> and <u>WJEC</u>, you'll have to write <u>two</u> non-fiction texts. For <u>OCR</u>, you only have to write <u>one</u> text.

> • The <u>question</u> will tell you the <u>type</u> of text to write, e.g. a newspaper report, a letter or a speech.
> • It'll usually tell you <u>who</u> you're writing for and <u>why</u> you're writing.

3) Have a look at Section 3 on pages 27-49 for more about answering writing questions.

You need to know what kind of English you're studying...

Exams definitely aren't much fun, but it's good to know what to <u>expect</u>. This page covers what you <u>need to know</u> if you're taking a GCSE English or English Language exam at Higher or Foundation level.

Planning

You've got to make a <u>plan</u> for <u>every essay</u> you write. That's a plan <u>on paper</u> — not in your head.

Decide what to say **Before** you start **Writing**

Think about what you're going to write <u>before</u> you start — that way your ideas will have a clear structure.

Good writing <u>makes a point</u>. It doesn't just ramble on about nothing.

In an exam, try to come up with <u>enough ideas</u> to keep you writing till your time's up.

Leave yourself about 5 minutes to check through your work though.

Stick your **Points** down on **Paper**

1) Before you start writing, spend about <u>5 minutes</u> jotting down a <u>plan</u> of the points you want to make.

2) Don't bother writing your plan in proper sentences.

> Q1   A local nature reserve is looking for part-time volunteers to help them out during the summer holidays. You decide to apply. Write your letter of application.
> Your letter should include: • who you are
>   • why you would like to volunteer
>   • why you think you're right for the job

If the question has bullet points make sure you include all of them in your answer.

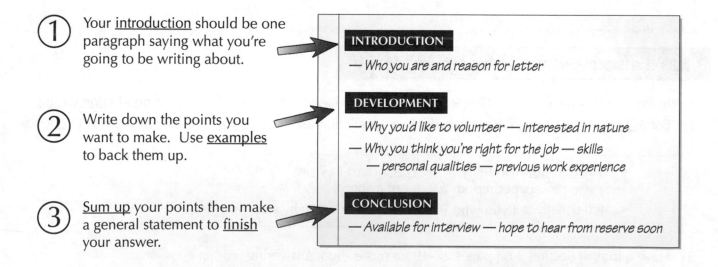

① Your <u>introduction</u> should be one paragraph saying what you're going to be writing about.

INTRODUCTION
— *Who you are and reason for letter*

② Write down the points you want to make. Use <u>examples</u> to back them up.

DEVELOPMENT
— *Why you'd like to volunteer — interested in nature*
— *Why you think you're right for the job — skills*
    — personal qualities — previous work experience

③ <u>Sum up</u> your points then make a general statement to <u>finish</u> your answer.

CONCLUSION
— *Available for interview — hope to hear from reserve soon*

A good plan means you won't be tempted to ramble in your essay...

Writing that <u>rambles on</u> without getting anywhere <u>isn't</u> going to get you good marks — it's a case of quality over quantity here. All this needs to be <u>second nature</u> by the time you get to the exam, so get <u>learning</u>.

Starting Your Answer

You need to write a <u>clear</u> and <u>punchy introduction</u> to your answer — no waffle allowed.

Start with a Good Introduction

Introduce the <u>overall point</u> that your essay is making — and do it clearly.

> The introduction gives a <u>brief answer</u> to the question. The rest of the essay goes into more <u>depth</u>, and gives <u>evidence</u> to back up your points.

Your introduction should Tell the reader What your essay is About

> 1. Compare the texts 'Antipodean Adventures' and 'My Journey Across Australia' using the following headings: • the presentation of the text
> • the layout of the text

Use <u>similar wording</u> to the question to link your answer to the question.

Explain the <u>effect</u> on the <u>reader</u>.

<u>'Antipodean Adventures' and 'My Journey Across Australia' both use presentation and layout for effect. 'Antipodean Adventures' uses bright colours to appeal to younger readers. 'My Journey Across Australia' has a more formal layout to suit its adult audience.</u>

<u>Clear</u> argument.

Use the introduction to Grab the Reader's Attention

Your first paragraph should make the reader want to read on, so make sure it's <u>interesting</u>.

> 2. Write an article for a magazine arguing against keeping wild animals in zoos.
> The article should include: • why you think that keeping wild animals in zoos is wrong
> • what should be done about it

<u>Imaginative</u> beginning to interest the reader.

Language appeals to the reader's <u>emotions</u>.

<u>Put yourself in his shoes</u>: you're the king of the jungle — <u>you should be running wild and free</u>. Instead you're pacing a <u>tiny concrete cell</u> with nothing to do but stare at the <u>blank walls</u>. <u>How would you feel? Yes we need to protect endangered animals</u>, but <u>shouldn't we find a better way?</u>

Refers to the <u>opposite point of view</u>.

Asks <u>questions</u> to draw the reader in.

Use the introduction to get the examiner on your side...

The introduction is the <u>very first thing</u> the examiner will read, and you want to impress them from the start. This means making sure your introduction is <u>clear</u>, <u>interesting</u> and <u>to the point</u>.

Paragraphs

Here's a little secret from me to you — <u>use paragraphs properly</u> if you want to get a decent grade.

Paragraphs make your writing Clearer

1) A <u>paragraph</u> is a group of sentences.
These sentences are usually about the same thing.

2) If you're answering a <u>reading</u> question, start a new paragraph every time you make a <u>new point</u>.

3) If you're writing <u>your own</u> text, start a new paragraph every time there's a <u>change</u>.
For example:

> You should use a new paragraph when you start writing about a <u>new topic</u>, <u>time</u> or <u>place</u>, or when a <u>new person speaks</u>, e.g. if you're putting a <u>quote</u> into a <u>newspaper article</u>.

> The writer uses shocking facts to show the effects of smoking. She states that it is a major cause of cancer.
> The writer also highlights the problem of obesity in society by using statistics and emotional language.

The <u>ideas</u> in this paragraph are all about <u>smoking</u>. The next part is about obesity — it's making a new point, so you need to start a <u>new paragraph</u>.

Paragraphs need to be Linked Together

Use words and phrases like these to make the link clear:

- Therefore...
- However...
- For the same reason...
- On the other hand...
- Again...

Try to vary the style of your paragraphs. See page 42 for some language techniques you could use.

These words clearly link the paragraphs together:

> ... free school meals for all pupils would mean that everyone got one healthy meal a day
> <u>However</u>, some people say that free school meals would be too expensive...

> ... people like the Scouts and yoga groups use the town hall every week.
> <u>Therefore</u>, I feel it would be a very bad idea to close the town hall...

Paragraphs should Follow a Clear Order

1) Make sure your paragraphs have a <u>clear order</u>.

2) It's up to you how you do it — just make sure it <u>makes sense</u>.

- Put your paragraphs in order of <u>importance</u>.
- Give paragraphs <u>for</u> an argument then paragraphs <u>against</u>.
- Put your paragraphs <u>in time order</u>.

Look at how other writers use paragraphs...

Try looking at some different pieces of writing, e.g. from a newspaper report or a website. Think about <u>why</u> the authors have used paragraphs where they have, and in that <u>particular order</u>.

Formal and Informal Language

As a general rule, use <u>formal language</u> unless you're writing to friends or young people.

Write in Formal Language

1) Use <u>formal language</u> to speak or write to people you <u>don't know</u>. This includes your <u>examiner</u>.
2) You should use <u>formal language</u> in most of your essays.
3) When you use formal language, be accurate and <u>to the point</u>. Don't be chatty — that means <u>no slang</u>:

> I reckon the writer wants you to big up his cause and show the government who's boss. ✗

> The writer aims to encourage the reader to support his cause and oppose the government's decision. ✓

4) Use correct <u>punctuation</u>, <u>grammar</u> and <u>spelling</u> (see Section 4).

5) If you're writing <u>about</u> another text, <u>don't</u> say "I" this and "I" that — just talk about the question, the text, the characters, the style, etc.

> ~~I think that~~ The pictures in the leaflet make the camp seem exciting. For example, ~~I believe that~~ the image of people playing football makes it seem like a fun, energetic activity.

Only use Informal Language when it Suits The Task

1) Use <u>informal language</u> if you're writing to <u>friends</u>, people you <u>know well</u> or <u>teenagers</u>. It's <u>chattier</u> and more <u>relaxed</u> than formal language, but it <u>doesn't</u> mean you can use <u>text speak</u>.
2) Here's an example from a talk for teenagers about the internet:

Informal language is more suited to this audience than formal language.

> ... I'm not saying the internet isn't useful, but <u>how many hours have you lost watching videos of barking cats and meowing dogs online when you really should have been researching your history project?</u>

You still need to use fancy writing tricks to get the marks though. This is a <u>rhetorical question</u> — see p.42.

You have to know how to use formal language...

So basically, you've almost always got to use <u>formal language</u> when you're writing in the exam. That means <u>proper</u> spelling, punctuation and grammar and absolutely <u>no slang</u>. It's what the examiner will expect.

Giving Evidence and Quoting

You have to give <u>evidence</u> for everything you say or you'll <u>miss out</u> on loads of marks.

Give an **Example** every time you make a **Point**

You've got to show that you know what you're talking about — give <u>examples</u> for what you write.

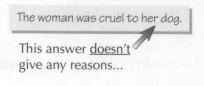

The woman was cruel to her dog.

This answer <u>doesn't</u> give any reasons...

...but this answer gives <u>examples</u> to back up the point it makes. That's loads better.

The woman was cruel to her dog. She kept him chained up in the sun all day, with very little food and no water.

Use **Quotes** from other people

1) <u>Quoting</u> means using someone else's words to back up your arguments.
2) To quote someone <u>in their own words</u>, put <u>quotation marks</u> (" ") around what they're saying. This separates the other person's words from yours.

The quotation marks separate <u>your</u> words...

...from <u>Mr. Wright's</u> words.

<u>Mr. Wright claimed that</u> "there was no other possible course of action."

Tips for using <u>quotation marks</u>:
- Use <u>exactly</u> the same words and punctuation as the person you're quoting.
- <u>Don't</u> make the quote <u>too long</u>.

3) If you put something <u>into your own words</u>, you don't need quotation marks:

Mrs. Fletcher says, "Reading greatly improves vocabulary."

Direct quote

Mrs. Fletcher claims that a good way to improve vocabulary is through reading.

In your own words

Writing must **Flow** around **Quotes**

Put your <u>quotes</u> in so the words around them still <u>make sense</u> and <u>flow</u> well:

Mr Jones said, "Getting children interested in drama is important to us." The board has agreed to pay for drama workshops.

"Quotes are great," said CGP...

Using loads of good <u>quotes</u> will definitely improve your grade. Just <u>remember</u>, when you're quoting to <u>support</u> a point you've made, you need to explain <u>why</u> your quote backs it up. See p.12 for more on this.

Concluding

You've got to <u>conclude</u> your answer — but it shouldn't be a last-minute rushed job.

Bring together the **Key Points** in your **Conclusion**

You need to be able to <u>finish off</u> your essay <u>properly</u> — and that means writing a good conclusion.

> 1. Write an article for a student magazine explaining why backpacking is popular as a form of travel.

1) Start a new paragraph and conclude by going back to the <u>question</u>.

2) Go over the <u>main points</u> of your answer. Don't add any <u>new points</u>. They should be in the <u>main part</u> of your essay.

> <u>For many people, backpacking is the best way to travel round</u> <u>different countries</u>. It lets you travel wherever you want, and it's great for <u>meeting interesting people</u>. It is also the <u>cheapest way</u> <u>of travelling</u>, so people are more likely to be able to afford a visit to places that are far away. <u>It's good to know that people don't need</u> <u>all their luxuries when they travel</u>.

3) Once you've summed up, write one last sentence to <u>finish</u>.

There are lots of **Different Ways** to **Conclude**

1) You could give <u>advice</u> about what to do next:

> ... we must do something. We need to create more protected areas of woodland before it's too late.

2) You could ask the reader a <u>rhetorical question</u> (see p.42):

> ... so, do we take action or just sit back and do nothing? Is this the end of the world as we know it?

This gives the reader a chance to make up their own mind.

3) You could <u>go back</u> to the points you made in your introduction.

4) If you're using <u>formal</u> language, you could start your last paragraph with 'In conclusion...'.

Plan your time carefully in the exam...

Always leave <u>time</u> to write your <u>conclusion</u>, even if it means writing less in the main bit of your answer. It's your chance to bring all your points <u>together</u> and show you've answered the <u>question</u>.

Checking

You've got five minutes left in the exam... time to <u>read through</u> your work.

Check Over your Answers when you've Finished

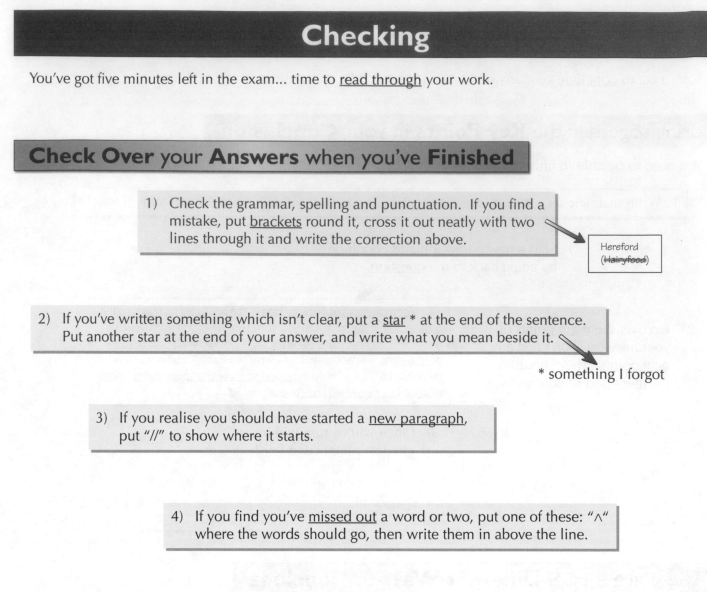

1) Check the grammar, spelling and punctuation. If you find a mistake, put <u>brackets</u> round it, cross it out neatly with two lines through it and write the correction above.

> Hereford
> (~~Hairyfood~~)

2) If you've written something which isn't clear, put a <u>star</u> * at the end of the sentence. Put another star at the end of your answer, and write what you mean beside it.

> * something I forgot

3) If you realise you should have started a <u>new paragraph</u>, put "//" to show where it starts.

4) If you find you've <u>missed out</u> a word or two, put one of these: "∧" where the words should go, then write them in above the line.

Don't Panic if you realise you've Gone Wrong in an Exam

If you realise you've <u>forgotten</u> something obvious, then add it in — even if it's at the bottom of the final page. You might get marks for noticing your mistake.

<u>Never cross out</u> your <u>whole answer</u> if you realise it's wrong. If you've got time left, explain what the <u>real answer</u> is.

Always chck yoor worke...

Mistakes are <u>easy to make</u>, especially in exam conditions, so you must give yourself <u>time</u> to check things over at the end. Don't panic if you realise you've gone wrong — just think about what you can do to <u>fix it</u>.

Revision Summary

Every now and then throughout this book, you'll find pages like this one.
They may look dull, but they're really important, so <u>don't skip them</u>.

- Try these questions and <u>tick off each one</u> when you <u>get it right</u>.
- When you've done <u>all the questions</u> for a topic and are <u>completely happy</u> with it, tick off the topic.

Planning (p2) ☑

1) How long (roughly) should you spend planning each essay in an exam? ☑

2) Your plan should cover the main three sections of your answer. The first of these sections is the introduction. What are the other two? ☑

Starting Your Answer (p3) ☑

3) Why would you use similar wording to the question in your introduction? ☑

4) How might your introduction grab the reader's attention? ☑

Paragraphs (p4) ☑

5) Why should you write your answers using paragraphs? ☑

6) Which of these would be a reason to start a new paragraph:
   a) when a new person speaks, b) when you make a new point, c) when you're hungry? ☑

7) Which of these words and phrases are generally good for linking paragraphs:
   a) However, b) I don't know, c) On the other hand, d) Horses? ☑

8) Which would be better — to order your paragraphs from longest to shortest or in order of importance? ☑

Formal and Informal Language (p5) ☑

9) Is formal language:
   a) accurate and chatty, b) accurate and to the point? ☑

10) Which of the following would you write in informal language:
    a) a letter to your MP, b) a postcard to your friend,
    c) an article on clothes for a teenage magazine? ☑

Giving Evidence and Quoting (p6) ☑

11) Why do you need to give examples for the points you make? ☑

12) What are quotation marks used for? ☑

13) Do you need to use quotation marks when you put what someone else has said into your own words? ☑

Concluding (p7) ☑

14) Which of these would make a good conclusion —
    a) advice about what to do next, b) a brand new point,
    c) a summary of the points you made in your introduction, d) your reader's horoscope? ☑

Checking (p8) ☑

15) What's the best thing to do if you realise that you've forgotten to include something important in your exam answer? ☑

16) Explain why you need to leave yourself time at the end of the exam to check through your answer. ☑

Reading the Question

A <u>non-fiction</u> text is anything that's about <u>real life</u>, like a newspaper article or a leaflet.

Three Things to get you Marks in Non-Fiction Text exams

These are all things that the examiner wants to give you marks for:

1) Showing that you've <u>understood</u> and thought about the texts, and that you can <u>compare</u> them.
2) Showing that you can pick out <u>facts</u> from the text and <u>explain</u> them.
3) Explaining how <u>language</u> and <u>how the text looks</u> can influence the reader.

<u>Don't panic</u> — this section will show you how to do all these things.

Read the Question Before the Text

Look at the question <u>before</u> you start — it'll tell you what to look out for.

Pick out the <u>key words</u> in each question and <u>underline</u> them.

1) <u>Compare</u> how the writers use <u>language</u> to <u>influence the reader</u> in 'The Future of Our Planet: Should We Be Building an Ark?' and 'End of the World? I don't think so.'

2) <u>What reasons</u> can you find in the newspaper article for saying that Jimmy Jones is both a <u>successful singer</u> and <u>a helpful person?</u>

Think about How Much the question is Worth

1) The questions are worth <u>different amounts</u> of marks.
   The number of marks for each question will be written on the exam paper.
2) Make sure you know what the <u>total number of marks</u> is.
   Then you can decide how much of the <u>total time</u> to spend on each question.
3) Don't spend <u>half</u> the exam answering a question worth <u>4 marks</u> if the next question's worth <u>8 marks</u>.

What's the question worth? — I'll give you £5 and a lemon bonbon...

Spend <u>less time</u> on questions that are worth <u>fewer marks</u> — pretty simple really. And remember, what the examiner really wants is for you to show that you've <u>understood the text</u>. Do that and you're laughing.

Reading the Text and Making Notes

<u>No one</u> likes making notes, but they stop you <u>rambling on</u> in your essays.

You might need to **Pick Out Facts** from the text

Questions which ask you to pick out facts only need <u>short answers</u>.

> 1) A question may ask you to <u>find</u> and <u>write down</u> some bits of information from the text.
> 2) <u>Read the question</u> really carefully and only write down things the question <u>asks for</u>.
> 3) Look at the <u>number of marks</u> the question is worth. This tells you <u>how many</u> facts to pick out.

For some questions, your answer booklet might have a blank <u>numbered list</u> for you to fill in —
if it does, don't leave any <u>spaces</u>.

Find the bits that **Answer** the **Question**

After you've read the question, go through each text at least <u>twice</u>, slowly and carefully.
Pick out the <u>important</u> bits that will help you <u>answer the question</u>.

What are the writer's <u>thoughts and feelings</u> towards Ben Kilham's approach?
Your answer should include:
- whether or not he agrees with it
- what other people think
- his overall impression.

Some questions won't give you bullet points like this.

GENTLE BEN

Most people try not to get too close to wild bears. Not Ben Kilham. When two injured bears were brought to his animal park, he brought them home and looked after them in his guest room. "<u>It didn't take long for them to trust me</u>," he says, "They used to follow me round the house." <u>Some experts worry that treating bears this way will make them too tame.</u> <u>However</u>, Kilham cared for three cubs last year and they now live happily in the animal park with the other bears.

Underline key points as you read and jot down some notes on the exam paper.

<u>Key point</u> — Includes Ben's own words — shows the writer thinks what Ben says is important and suggests he agrees with him.

<u>Key point</u> — Shows what other people think about Ben's approach — makes the article seem more balanced.

<u>Key point</u> — The writer provides another argument which supports Ben's approach.

Make sure your answers focus on the question...

The examiner wants to know you've <u>understood</u> the text. When you're picking points out, make sure you're <u>only</u> writing down things that the question <u>asks for</u>. Other stuff's just a waste of time.

Longer Answers

The next two pages will give you the skills you'll need to write <u>longer</u>, more <u>detailed</u> answers.

Try to sound Confident

Use your own words to explain the question and then say what your argument's going to be.

Key words

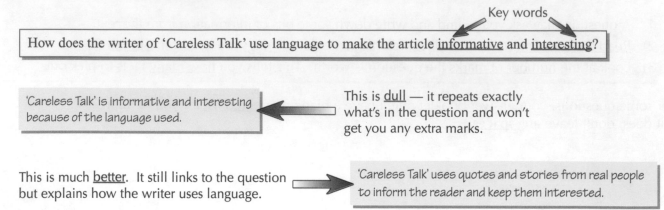

How does the writer of 'Careless Talk' use language to make the article <u>informative</u> and <u>interesting</u>?

'Careless Talk' is informative and interesting because of the language used.

This is <u>dull</u> — it repeats exactly what's in the question and won't get you any extra marks.

This is much <u>better</u>. It still links to the question but explains how the writer uses language.

'Careless Talk' uses quotes and stories from real people to inform the reader and keep them interested.

Back up your points with Examples

1) For questions that need longer answers, back up your points with <u>evidence</u>.
2) This will usually be a <u>quote</u> (see p.6), but it could be a description of the pictures or layout.
3) <u>Explain</u> what your example shows about the text.

These examples are about the <u>presentation</u> of the text.

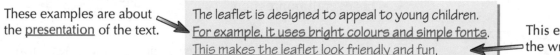

The leaflet is designed to appeal to young children. <u>For example, it uses bright colours and simple fonts</u>. <u>This makes the leaflet look friendly and fun</u>.

This explains <u>why</u> the writer chose a certain <u>style</u>.

So, here's what a good essay answer should do:

1) Make <u>points</u> to answer the question you've been given.
2) Give <u>examples</u> from the text (either a quote or a description).
3) <u>Explain</u> how your examples back up your point.

This is really important — keep <u>developing</u> your answer.

Don't bury examiners with too much detail...

EXAM TIP You should definitely try to back up your argument with <u>examples</u>, and add an <u>explanation</u>. But the examiner can always spot <u>waffle</u> — just <u>stick to the point</u>, and you'll get lots of marks.

Longer Answers

There are <u>plenty</u> of ways you can <u>develop</u> your answer — there's <u>more</u> to it than adding quotes.

Some questions ask about **Thoughts** and **Feelings**

You may understand the facts a writer gives you, but some questions will ask for <u>more</u>.

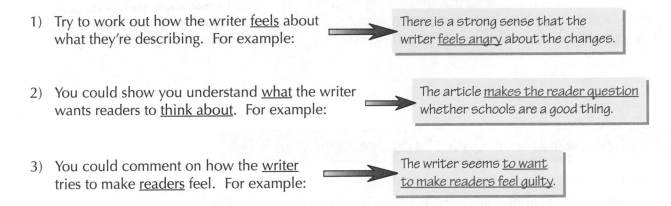

1) Try to work out how the writer <u>feels</u> about what they're describing. For example:

> There is a strong sense that the writer <u>feels angry</u> about the changes.

2) You could show you understand <u>what</u> the writer wants readers to <u>think about</u>. For example:

> The article <u>makes the reader question</u> whether schools are a good thing.

3) You could comment on how the <u>writer</u> tries to make <u>readers</u> feel. For example:

> The writer seems <u>to want to make readers feel guilty</u>.

Some questions will ask about the writer's language — there's more about this in <u>Section 3</u>.

Compare and **Contrast** the texts

1) You might get a question asking you to <u>compare</u> texts. This means picking out the <u>differences</u> and <u>similarities</u> between them. E.g.:

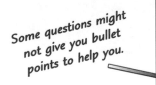

Some questions might not give you bullet points to help you.

> Now look again at all three items.
> They have each been written in an interesting way.
>
> **1.** Choose **two** of these items. Compare them using these headings:
> - the writers' intended audiences
> - the ways in which the writers use language.

2) If you're given <u>headings</u> or <u>bullet points</u>, write about all of them and write about the <u>same amount</u> for each.

3) <u>Plan</u> your answer before you start. If you're given <u>headings</u>, include points about each one in your <u>plan</u>.

4) Try to write an <u>equal amount</u> about both texts. Keep <u>making links</u> between them in your answer.

Writers write that way for a reason...

Some reading questions will ask you to consider less obvious things like the <u>writer's thoughts</u> and <u>ideas</u>. Be <u>confident</u> — if you think the writer feels a certain way, say so and then find some <u>evidence</u> to back it up.

Writing about the Format of a Non-Fiction Text

There's <u>lots</u> to think about when it comes to non-fiction texts, including the way the text <u>looks</u>.

It's **Not Just Words** you need to think about

1) The <u>texts</u> in the exam could be magazine or newspaper articles, or printed adverts.

2) You need to comment on the <u>format</u> of what you're given
— think about things like the overall <u>presentation</u>,
the <u>layout</u> of the text and the way <u>graphics</u> are used.

'Format' means the way the writing and pictures are organised to make a text look a certain way.

Think about what the **Graphics** are trying to **Do**

1) Texts often have graphics, e.g. photos, pictures, diagrams.
2) They might have <u>captions</u> with them — a short bit of text to explain what the graphic shows.
3) All graphics have a <u>purpose</u>, e.g. photos can show <u>real-life</u> examples of what's in the text. It's no good just saying that there are three photos. Instead <u>describe</u> them and <u>explain</u> their effect.

Mention the **Layout**

Different layouts are used for different <u>audiences</u>.

This layout is <u>serious</u>. There's hardly any colour, most of the text is the same size and the picture is formal. It's probably aimed at <u>adults</u>.

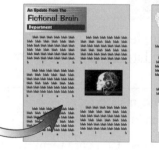

This layout is more <u>fun</u>. There's lots of colour, more space, the text size is varied, the picture is more entertaining. It's aimed at <u>young people</u>.

Talk about **Headlines** too

1) Headlines tell you <u>what</u> the article is <u>about</u> in a few words. They're there to grab your <u>attention</u>, so you'll read the article.
2) Headlines are usually <u>bigger</u> and at the <u>top</u> of the page.
3) They can use <u>humour</u> or <u>shocking facts</u> to get your attention.

This is the headline.

Learn these features and what they're used for...

Make sure you know <u>which</u> parts of the text are <u>which</u>. Then practise spotting the way different texts are formatted — try to explain what their <u>purpose</u> is and what their <u>effect</u> is on the reader.

Warm-Up Questions

People often find non-fiction texts a bit tricky, but if you've paid attention to this section, these warm-up questions should be OK. When you've warmed up, there are some bigger beasts for you to try — practice exam questions. The Foundation-level questions and sources are on pages 16-19, and the Higher-level ones are on pages 21-24. We've even thrown in one worked exam answer for each level too — you can find these on pages 20 and 25.

Warm-Up Questions

1) Is it best to read the question before or after you read the text? Why?

2) How can you make it really obvious that you're answering the question in your first sentence?

3) Look at the internet dating website below. How does the use of colour help the website to achieve its purpose?

4) What do we learn from the website about what Lonely Hearts Club hopes to achieve and why? Try to pick out at least three separate points.

5) How do the graphics help the website to achieve its purpose?

6) The passage below is taken from the 'About Us' section of another dating website. Write a short paragraph about the differences in how the two websites are written.

   "*Don't sit at home alone, sad and blue. There's always someone who's just right for you! That's right, girlfriends, there's no need to panic about who you're taking to the leavers' ball this year. Send in a catchy description and photograph of yourself and I, your very own Stupid Cupid, will search heaven and earth for your perfect boy. Bliss!*"

Now it's time for some exam-style questions — the sources for these questions are on pages 17-19. There's also a worked answer to question 4 on page 20, which should give you some good ideas about how to answer questions on non-fiction texts.

Read **Item 1**, the website article called 'Fireworks and animals', and answer the questions below.

1. List four things the leaflet tells you about how to prepare for bonfire night if you have animals.

(4 marks)

2. According to the article, why is it important to look after animals on bonfire night?

(4 marks)

Read **Item 2**, the newspaper article called 'British teenager becomes youngest person to sail round the world solo', and answer the question below.

3. What reasons can you find in the article for saying that Mike Perham had both "amazing" experiences and difficult times during his expedition?

(8 marks)

Read **Item 3**, the Habitat for Humanity article called 'When Danger Starts at Home', and answer the question below.

4. How does the writer use language to inform the reader and persuade them to donate money?

(12 marks)

Now look again at all three items. They have each been presented in an interesting way.

5. Choose **two** of these items. Compare them using these headings:

    •   the use of titles and subtitles
    •   the use of pictures.

(12 marks)

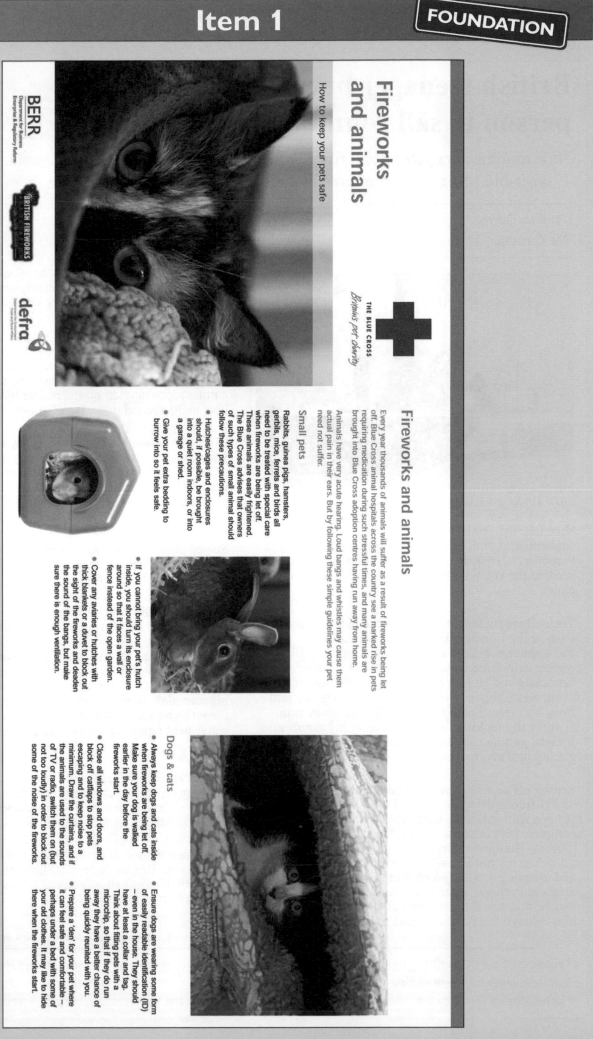

Fireworks and animals

How to keep your pets safe

THE BLUE CROSS
Britain's pet charity

BERR
Department for Business
Enterprise & Regulatory Reform

BRITISH FIREWORKS

defra
Department for
Environment, Food and Rural Affairs

Fireworks and animals

Every year thousands of animals will suffer as a result of fireworks being let off. Blue Cross animal hospitals across the country see a marked rise in pets requiring medication during such stressful times, and many animals are brought into Blue Cross adoption centres having run away from home.

Animals have very acute hearing. Loud bangs and whistles may cause them actual pain in their ears. But by following these simple guidelines your pet need not suffer.

Small pets

Rabbits, guinea pigs, hamsters, gerbils, mice, ferrets and birds all need to be treated with special care when fireworks are being let off. These animals are easily frightened. The Blue Cross advises that owners of such types of small animal should follow these precautions.

- Hutches/cages and enclosures should, if possible, be brought into a quiet room indoors, or into a garage or shed.

- Give your pet extra bedding to burrow into so it feels safe.

- If you cannot bring your pet's hutch inside, you should turn its enclosure around so that it faces a wall or fence instead of the open garden.

- Cover any aviaries or hutches with thick blankets or a duvet to block out the sight of the fireworks and deaden the sound of the bangs, but make sure there is enough ventilation.

- Close all windows and doors, and block off catflaps to stop pets escaping and to keep noise to a minimum. Draw the curtains, and if the animals are used to the sounds of TV or radio, switch them on (but not too loudly) in order to block out some of the noise of the fireworks.

Dogs & cats

- Always keep dogs and cats inside when fireworks are being let off. Make sure your dog is walked earlier in the day before the fireworks start.

- Ensure dogs are wearing some form of easily readable identification (ID) – even in the house. They should have at least a collar and tag. Think about fitting pets with a microchip, so that if they do run away they have a better chance of being quickly reunited with you.

- Prepare a 'den' for your pet where it can feel safe and comfortable – perhaps under a bed with some of your old clothes. It may like to hide there when the fireworks start.

Item 2

British teenager becomes youngest person to sail round the world solo

Nine months after setting sail from Portsmouth in his Open 50 racing yacht, 17-year-old Mike Perham returns home

Caroline Davies

The Guardian, 27 August 2009

Mike Perham on his return to Portsmouth

Nine months, some 30,000 miles, and several euphemistic* "Oh crikey!" moments after leaving Portsmouth, British teenager Mike Perham, 17, today became the youngest person to sail solo around the globe.

The college student from land-locked Hertfordshire crossed the finishing line between Lizard Point and Ushant in France at 9.47am after braving 50ft waves, gale-force winds and a couple of hair-raising "knockdowns" during his voyage into the record books. "I am absolutely ecstatic*. It feels amazing," he said from his Open 50 racing yacht, TotallyMoney.com. "I am really looking forward to seeing my family and friends, getting back to my own house, and especially getting into my own bed at last."

Setting off as a 16-year-old, equipped with an iPod, "icky" freeze-dried food supplies and a couple of robust laptops from which to blog, Mike's intention was to complete his circumnavigation* non-stop in under five months. But those hairy moments, which saw his auto-pilot then his rudder fail, winds that shredded his sail and towering waves, forced him to pull in for repairs. Stops in Portugal, Gran Canaria, Cape Town, Tasmania and New Zealand threw him behind schedule and forced him through the Panama Canal rather than round Cape

Horn. It also meant he had to abandon his attempt at a non-stop, non-assisted circumnavigation. "It was a bit of a disappointment. But I always knew there was a chance of stopping," he said.

Horrendous weather in the Southern Ocean saw 50ft waves in 50-knot winds, and necessitated mast repairs after two knockdowns*. Another drama found him cutting ropes tangled on the rudder by diving under the boat in 30-second dives for 40 minutes in the Pacific.

"There are lows, but the ongoing low is that you are on your own, totally," he said yesterday via satellite phone. "That's not nice, but it is part of the challenge. I never thought about giving up. Though sometimes you do ask yourself, Why on earth am I doing it?

"There were so many experiences I will never forget. Seeing hundreds of dolphins at once, or seeing whales next to you. There were some incredible sunsets and some beautifully clear days."

Sleeping in half-hour snatches, he avoided pirates in the Caribbean by turning off his tracking system, and dodged tankers around Panama, while continuing his studies for a sports diploma. Twice daily satellite calls to his father, Peter, 49, his mother, Heather, 51, and his sister, Fiona, 18, at home in Potters Bar helped ease his solitude*. With his iPod on shuffle, and featuring favourite bands U2 and the Black Eyed Peas, his days were spent repairing, and stuffing himself with rice and pasta.

He cracked open champagne twice – on his 17th birthday on 16 March, and on crossing the equator. It is not his first record. At 14 he became the youngest to cross the Atlantic single-handed.

His father, who joined him today, said: "Mike is a very special son. He has done incredibly well and shown that with determination you can succeed in the most adverse* circumstances."

---

*euphemistic — describing upsetting words in a more polite way

*circumnavigation — a sailing voyage around the world

*knockdowns — when a boat is knocked over so that it lies flat in the water

* solitude — loneliness

* adverse — difficult

* ecstatic — very happy

When Danger Starts at Home

Please help me get families like Hector's out of the derelict apartments and into decent homes – for good.

Hector lives in "La Boca", a dangerous neighbourhood in the City of Buenos Aires. Home for Hector's family is a crumbling, rusting apartment block with his dad Jorge, his mum Estela, his sisters Claudia and Viviana (eleven year old twins) and brother Victor.

The very structure of the apartment block is dangerous and a tragedy waiting to happen. Every step you take is followed by a cracking sound and Jorge has to warn his youngest son not to jump inside the house. Why? Because he might go through the floor.

The family faces many dangers each day, just from living in the apartment block. The neighbourhood is full of such tenement* buildings, all of which are prone to fires.

© Oliver Kornblihtt

Hector's family has to be very careful with the lights and gas supply because the building is so dilapidated*. One mistake could mean the destruction of the whole structure, or worse.

Why do so many families like Hector's live amid such daily dangers? Because they have no choice.

There is a massive housing deficit* in Argentina, and thousands upon thousands of families have no choices except living on the street, in abandoned factories, or in derelict apartments.

These derelict apartments come with a price beyond the danger. Because they are in such poor condition, it is illegal to let them out, so their unscrupulous* owners take advantage of desperate families. There are no terms; there is no legal recourse*; and the families have no leg to stand on. But they are desperate so they pay the money, knowing full well that they might be evicted at any moment.

So the choice really is: do you want your family to live on the streets, or not? Is it better to risk life in this apartment than life on the streets?

Thankfully, this terrible choice can come to an end. There is another way for these families. Together we can offer more and more families in these illegal and rundown apartments a way out. We need your help to renovate the future for hundreds of families like Hector's.

You can be a part of this solution for Hector and hundreds of others like him. Your gift will help us transform the lives of families like Hector's. Hector's family should not have to suffer the dangers of a crumbling, rotting apartment; what they need is a safe, decent home.

---

*tenement — a run-down apartment block

*dilapidated — run down

*deficit — shortage

*unscrupulous — unfair

*legal recourse — getting the law to help

FOUNDATION Worked Exam Answer

To help you get to grips with these non-fiction reading texts exam questions, I've cooked up a little exam answer to give you some pointers. Enjoy.

Read **Item 3**, the Habitat for Humanity article called 'When Danger Starts at Home' and answer the question below.

4. How does the writer use language to inform the reader and persuade them to donate money?

(12 marks)

Inform

This article uses informative language to show how bad things are for Hector and his family, and for thousands of people like him, and how we can act to help them. By focusing on one family the writer can show the problems that they face, while talking about a problem that affects "thousands" of people. This makes it <u>easier for the reader to understand how the problem affects people</u>.

Try to show how the language used helps to inform the reader.

The writer uses technical language to describe the situation, for example "housing deficit" and "legal recourse". This tells the reader facts about the situation and how serious it is. It also makes the writer seem well informed.

The writer makes it clear to the reader that their help is needed, by using words like <u>"you" and "we"</u>. This makes it clear that the main purpose of the article is to show how the reader can help people like Hector, for example by referring to "your help" and "your gift".

When you're writing about the language, mention the particular words used.

Persuade

The writer uses <u>emotive</u> language to show that the housing problem in Buenos Aires affects individuals. He does this by telling the story of one family. By giving details of the family members such as names and ages, we are made to sympathise with them directly and want to donate money to help improve their living conditions.

'Emotive' is a good word — it means it's trying to get the reader to feel strongly.

The writer uses vivid descriptive language to describe the family living in "<u>a crumbling, rusting apartment block</u>". This helps the reader to picture how bad it is, which makes us feel sorry for them and want to help.

Try to put in a short quote for nearly every point.

The writer describes their home as "a tragedy waiting to happen." This dramatic language makes it seem like helping them is really urgent, as if something terrible might happen if they don't move into better housing. <u>This means the reader is more likely to donate money straight away</u>.

Think about what effect the language will have on the reader.

Exam Questions

Now it's time for some exam questions that are more like the ones you'll get in a Higher tier paper. The sources for these questions are on pages 22-24, and there's a worked answer to a question on Item 1 on page 25 to give you an idea of what the examiners are looking for.

Read **Item 1**, the leaflet about the charity Plan International and their 'Sponsor a Child' campaign.

1. What do you find out from the leaflet about Plan International and the ways that they help children in poor communities?

    (8 marks)

Now read **Item 2**, the magazine article entitled *Destination New York*.

2. How does the presentation of the article add to its effectiveness?

    (8 marks)

Now read **Item 3**, an extract from John Krakauer's *Into the Wild*.

3. What are the narrator's thoughts and feelings about climbing Devil's Thumb?

    (8 marks)

Now you need to refer to **Item 3**, *Into the Wild*, and **either** Item 1 **or** Item 2.

4. Compare the ways in which the writers use language to achieve their purpose in the two texts.

    (16 marks)

Make a child's future part of your plans.

Children in the world's poorest countries have hopes, dreams and plans for the future – just like the rest of us. But without your help, these children might never see their plans made a reality. In fact, they might not have a future at all.

PLAN INTERNATIONAL

The Plan that fights poverty

In some countries where we work, one in five children will die before their fifth birthday. Those who survive can face lives of incredible hardship. They are weakened by hunger and easily preventable diseases. They are denied the education that could lift them out of poverty and give them a future of opportunity. We believe that this is wrong. It is unjust. And we have a plan to change things.

The Plan that changes lives

Sponsor a child and you'll become part of a very special plan – a plan that will transform their life and yours. You'll help provide communities with clean water, nourishing food, healthcare and education. So you'll touch not just one child's life, but the lives of their families, friends and neighbours too.

The Plan you can see in action

The child you sponsor will be your window into another world. Right from day one, you can build a unique one-to-one relationship. And over time, you'll watch them grow and see how your support is helping to change their life and the lives of those around them. When you start to sponsor a child, you'll receive a Welcome Pack. The pack includes a photo and details of the child you are sponsoring, as well as information on the types of projects you're funding in the country where they live. If you wish, you can send personal messages to encourage the child you sponsor – and you'll receive messages in return that will inspire you and your family. Some sponsors even go and visit. But however you choose to get involved, you can be sure that you'll find it a rewarding and fascinating experience.

Photo: Plan International/Martin Edstrom

Photo: Plan International/Rob Few   Photo: Plan International/Jiro Ose

The Plan you can trust

Plan International pioneered child sponsorship over 75 years ago. Today, over 80,000 people in the UK alone sponsor children with us.

Throughout our history, we've put children at the very heart of our work to end poverty – giving them the skills and knowledge they need to make the most of their lives. It's a plan that works – and a plan that you'll see in action through messages from the child you sponsor and updates on the work you're helping to fund in their country.

The Plan that works: Filifing's story

Photo: Plan International

Filifing always wanted to be a nurse. But her dream might never have come true without her Plan International sponsor, whose donations helped build a new school for her village and whose messages of encouragement inspired Filifing.

Today, Filifing works at her local health centre. She's proud of her job, and a great role model for girls in her community. She's living proof that the cycle of poverty can be broken. And you can imagine how pleased her sponsor must be that Filifing has put her plans into action.

Right now, many more children need your support. Please sponsor a child with Plan International UK.

Travel

Destination
NEW YORK

The *Easy Living* fashion team took Manhattan for our April shoot, *Gallery Girl*. And their stay in the Big Apple was made all the more glamorous by staying at the oh-so-stylish Sofitel New York

BY CHARLOTTE JOLLY

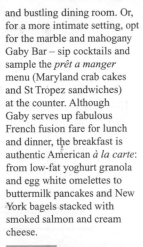

Clockwise from right: a model showcases classic NYC style; the elegant New York Public Library; the stunning New York skyline from Central Park.

If your trip is all about location, location, location, then you can't top the towering Manhattan outpost of French hotel chain Sofitel, on West 44th Street. Its address (otherwise known as Club Row thanks to the presence of the New York Yacht Club, Harvard Club and other prestigious Ivy League associations) ensures the hotel is not encircled by touring parties, and the block is distinguished by fluttering flags rather than flashing neon lights. However, Fifth Avenue, Times Square and Broadway are just a few blocks away, and you can stroll over to world-famous museums and make your reservations at exclusive eateries in just a few precious New York minutes. Despite its stellar spot midtown, Sofitel New York specialises in quiet luxury and civilised calm.

SLEEP The French connection extends to the rooms and suites; the walls are adorned with Parisian cityscapes, and elegant marble bathrooms are decorated with orchids and stocked with L'Occitane toiletries. Yet the spaciousness, 24-hour room service and suites equipped with two televisions are the epitome of American comfort and luxury. The outlook from the rooms' floor-to-ceiling windows varies, but, once you climb to around the 18th floor, there are open views over the city that

never sleeps. Le Fitness, the hotel's gym, is open around the clock, but we recommend an early morning run through Bryant Park and on to Central Park.

TO DO First stop has to be a Broadway show. Pop down to any of the ticket-selling booths around Times Square for the best discounts. Next, hit Fifth Avenue for NYC shopping mainstays (from Bergdorf Goodman to Banana Republic), and if that takes its toll on your credit card, we thoroughly recommend the free tours of the New York Public Library. Another top tourist tip is the New York City Pass – it grants you access to six of New York's most popular attractions and costs 45 per cent less

than individually purchased tickets. Your pass gets you into the Guggenheim, the Museum Of Modern Art, the Met and the Empire State Building Observatory – and all of these attractions are within walking distance of the hotel.

EAT AND DRINK Installed in Sofitel's 30-storey glass and limestone tower is Gaby restaurant, a glamorous, Art Deco-inspired, street-side brasserie. Sit down to hearty omelet bordelaise or fresh seared yellow fin tuna Nicoise salad in the bright

and bustling dining room. Or, for a more intimate setting, opt for the marble and mahogany Gaby Bar – sip cocktails and sample the *prêt a manger* menu (Maryland crab cakes and St Tropez sandwiches) at the counter. Although Gaby serves up fabulous French fusion fare for lunch and dinner, the breakfast is authentic American *à la carte*: from low-fat yoghurt granola and egg white omelettes to buttermilk pancakes and New York bagels stacked with smoked salmon and cream cheese.

BOOK IT Prices start from £193 per room per night, based on two adults sharing a standard double room, on a room-only basis. For more information and reservations, call 00 1 212 354-8844 or email sofitel.newyork@sofitel.com.

HIGHER

Item 3

In this extract, Jon Krakauer attempts a solo climb of Devils Thumb mountain in Alaska.

Into the Wild
by Jon Krakauer

[handwritten: gaps]

[handwritten: wall supporting]

On the afternoon of May 15, when the blizzard finally abated, I returned to the southeast face and climbed to the top of a slender ridge that abuts the upper peak like a flying buttress* on a Gothic cathedral. I decided to spend the night there, on the narrow crest, sixteen hundred feet below the summit. The evening sky was cold and cloudless. I could see all the way to tidewater and beyond. At dusk I watched, transfixed, as the lights of Petersburg blinked on in the west. The closest thing I'd had to human contact since the airdrop, the distant lights triggered a flood of emotion that caught me off guard. I imagined people watching baseball on television, eating fried chicken in brightly lit kitchens, drinking beer, making love. When I lay down to sleep, I was overcome by a wrenching loneliness. I'd never felt so alone, ever.

That night I had troubled dreams, of a police bust and vampires and a gangland-style execution. I heard someone whisper, "I think he's in there...." I sat bolt upright and opened my eyes. The sun was about to rise. The entire sky was scarlet. It was still clear, but a thin, wispy scum of cirrus* had spread across the upper atmosphere, and a dark line of squalls was visible just above the southwestern horizon. I pulled on my boots and hurriedly strapped on my crampons*. Five minutes after waking up I was climbing away from the bivouac*.

[handwritten: top of mountain]

I carried no rope, no tent or bivouac gear, no hardware save my ice axes. My plan was to go light and fast, to reach the summit and make it back down before the weather turned. Pushing myself, continually out of breath, I scurried up and to the left, across small snowfields linked by ice-choked clefts and short rock steps. The climbing was almost fun — the rock was covered with large, incut holds, and the ice, though thin, never got steeper than seventy degrees — but I was anxious about the storm front racing in from the Pacific, darkening the sky.

I didn't have a watch, but in what seemed like a very short time, I was on the distinctive final ice field. By now the entire sky was smeared with clouds. It looked easier to keep angling to the left but quicker to go straight for the top. Anxious about being caught by a storm high on the peak and without shelter, I opted for the direct route. The ice steepened and thinned. I swung my left ice ax and struck rock. I aimed for another spot, and once again it glanced off unyielding diorite with a dull clank. And again, and again. It was a reprise of my first attempt on the north face. Looking between my legs, I stole a glance at the glacier more than two thousand feet below. My stomach churned.

[handwritten: fearful.]

*flying buttress — a half-arch structure that supports the wall of a building
*cirrus — a type of thin cloud
*crampons — metal frames with spikes, attached to boots to help with grip in snow and ice
*bivouac — a temporary, usually improvised, campsite or shelter

*[handwritten: climbing a mountain
- at first he is determined
- then he feels alone
- anxious
- hes terrified]*

Worked Exam Answer

Getting top marks in your answers to non-fiction reading questions isn't easy.
Check out this sample exam answer for tips on how to really impress the examiner.

---

1. Read **Item 1** on page 22, the leaflet about the charity Plan International and their 'Sponsor a Child' campaign.

   How do the presentational features used in Item 1 help to make the text more effective?

   (8 marks)

   <u>Essay plan</u>

   1) Intro — different presentational features used to inform and persuade

   2) Photos — happy children, show charity's good work

   3) Subheadings — summarise info, show key ideas

   4) Different colours — contrasting, help reader remember key messages

   5) Conclusion — summarise main points, link back to purpose

   The charity leaflet for the 'Sponsor a Child' campaign tries to inform readers about the difficult lives of children around the world and persuade them to donate money by sponsoring these children. <u>It uses a number of presentational features to achieve these aims, including photographs, subheadings and different colours.</u>

   Outline what presentational features are used and why in your introduction.

   The photos at the top of the leaflet are used to persuade the reader to sponsor a child. <u>The pictures show children smiling or laughing</u>, which shows that the charity is successful at improving children's lives. This has a persuasive effect on the reader, because they feel that by donating they could make more children happy like the children in the photos.

   When you're talking about presentation, your example is normally a description.

   <u>The leaflet also uses a number of subheadings to help inform the reader. The subheadings, such as "The Plan you can trust", summarise the content of each paragraph. This makes the leaflet more effective at informing the reader, because by reading the subheadings the reader can instantly find out the key ideas that the text is trying to convey.</u>

   Remember to include a point, an example and an explanation of the point somewhere in each paragraph.

   Colour is used to make key parts of the text memorable to the reader. For example, the colour green is used to emphasise the text at the bottom of the leaflet, which contains some of the text's key messages — that children in poor communities need "support" and that the reader should "sponsor a child". <u>The green colour contrasts with the black text and the blue text box nearby, which makes it stand out to the reader. This ensures that they will read and remember these key messages,</u> which supports the text's overall purpose of persuading more people to sponsor a child.

   Think about the effect of different presentational features.

   In summary, the leaflet uses several presentational features to effectively achieve its aims. Subheadings make the information clear to the reader, while photos and colour make the text more persuasive by showing the positive effects of donating and helping the reader remember the text's key messages.

   Sum up your points in a brief conclusion.

Revision Summary

Have a go at these questions on <u>Section Two</u>. If you get stuck, don't worry, just go back and read that page again, then <u>have another go</u> at the question. Don't forget to <u>tick off each topic</u> once you're happy with it.

Reading the Question (p10) ☑

1) What should you underline in an exam question? ☑
2) Is there any point in thinking about how many marks the whole paper is worth? Why? ☑

Reading the Text and Making Notes (p11) ☑

3) If a question asks you to pick out some facts from the text, why is it important to look at the number of marks the question is worth? ☑

4) Explain why it's important to read through the text slowly and make a few notes before you start thinking about how to start your essay. ☑

Longer Answers (p12-13) ☑

5) In the introduction to your answer should you:
   a) use the exact same words as the question, b) reword and develop the question? ☑

6) When you make a point in an essay, what should you back it up with:
   a) nothing — you don't have the time
   b) examples from the text
   c) a comfortable cushion? ☑

7) Other than facts, what else could you think about when writing about a text:
   a) how the writer feels about the subject
   b) what you think they had for breakfast
   c) what the writer wants the reader to think about? ☑

8) If you're asked to compare and contrast, what should you do:
   a) write about the similarities and differences between the texts
   b) just write about one text in detail and ignore the other one
   c) draw the examiner a pretty picture? ☑

Writing about the Format of a Non-Fiction Text (p14) ☑

9) What is meant by the 'format' of a text? ☑
10) List three different kinds of graphics that you might find in a non-fiction text. ☑
11) What is the purpose of a caption? ☑
12) Briefly describe an example of each of the following (you can do a diagram if you want):
   a) effective use of layout on a newsletter aimed at teenagers.
   b) ineffective use of layout on a newsletter aimed at teenagers. ☑
13) What is the main purpose of a headline? How does it achieve this purpose? ☑

Different Forms

Non-fiction texts come in many <u>different forms</u>. The next two pages cover the main ones.

Letters can be **Formal** or **Informal**

1) <u>Informal letters</u> are the kind of letters that you'd send to a friend.
   Use a <u>chatty style</u> if it suits the reader, but stick to <u>Standard English</u> (see p.51).
2) <u>Formal letters</u>, e.g. job applications, need a more <u>serious</u> tone and language.
3) Give letters a clear <u>structure</u>, e.g. a greeting at the beginning and a suitable ending.
4) Letters can have many different <u>purposes</u> (see p.30). E.g.:

> • <u>informing</u> — gives readers information, e.g. a letter to a newspaper about a fund-raising event.
>
> • <u>persuading</u> — gets someone to do something, e.g. a letter to a friend persuading them to visit you.

Newspaper and **Magazine** articles should be **Factual**

For <u>newspaper</u> or <u>magazine articles</u>, you only need to write the <u>text</u>, so don't worry about <u>layout</u>.

1) You need to give <u>facts</u> and <u>evidence</u> — e.g. quotes (see p.6) and statistics.
2) Use <u>headlines</u> and <u>subheadings</u> to break up the writing so it's easier to read.
3) Articles can have different <u>purposes</u>, e.g.:

Articles can have more than one purpose.

> • <u>informing</u> — e.g. a newspaper article telling people about an upcoming event.
>
> • <u>explaining</u> — e.g. a car magazine might explain the features of a new family car.

The <u>language</u> and <u>tone</u> of an article depends on its <u>purpose</u> and <u>audience</u>.

Leaflets are usually short

Leaflets can <u>inform</u>, <u>advise</u> or put across an <u>argument</u>.

1) If you're writing a leaflet, don't spend <u>time</u> making it look <u>pretty</u> or drawing <u>pictures</u>.
2) Leaflets should <u>catch people's attention</u> and <u>give information</u> clearly.
3) Use <u>headings</u> and <u>bullet points</u> to break up the text.
4) This is the <u>kind</u> of question you could get:

> Write the text of a leaflet which informs tourists of what your area has to offer them.

I'll keep this short and sweet — revise...

Letters, newspaper or magazine articles and leaflets can be about <u>almost anything</u> at all. If you have to write one of these texts in the exam, <u>read the question</u> carefully to find out <u>who</u> you're writing for, and <u>why</u>.

Different Forms

You want <u>more types</u> of non-fiction text — you've come to the right place.

Reviews are Round-Ups of information

<u>Reviews</u> describe something, e.g. a film, and say what is (or isn't) great about it.

1) Reviews can be <u>formal</u> or <u>informal</u>. Their purpose is to <u>inform</u> (see p.30) and give an <u>opinion</u>.
2) <u>Include some facts</u> — your audience needs to know <u>exactly</u> what it is you're writing about.
3) Write <u>confidently</u>. Show your audience that you know what you're talking about.

> For example, you might write a <u>review</u> of:
> - a hotel
> - a restaurant
> - a book
> - a play or film

Talks and Speeches are designed to be Spoken

For talks or speeches you need to make the words <u>easy to remember</u>.

> 1) Write in a style that would <u>sound good</u> to a room full of listeners.
> 2) The tone might be <u>formal</u> or <u>informal</u> (see p.5), depending on your audience.
> 3) Include some <u>interesting language</u> and <u>techniques</u> (see p.42).
> 4) Give your speech a <u>clear structure</u>, e.g. <u>start with a short introduction</u> to the topic and <u>finish by reminding</u> the audience what they've just been told.

Make your writing Organised and Interesting

Whatever form of text you're writing, you'll be marked on:

> - how well you <u>organise</u> and <u>communicate</u> the information.
> - the <u>quality</u> of your <u>writing</u>.

1) <u>Structure</u> your writing using <u>paragraphs</u> and link your <u>sentences</u> together.
2) <u>Sometimes</u> you can you use headings and bullet points, but make sure you write mostly in paragraphs.
3) Write in a way that'll <u>interest</u> your readers.

You need to know about the features of <u>different forms</u>...

Jot down from memory the <u>key features</u> of each different type of text. Think about what <u>style of writing</u> would be most suitable for each form. Then practise writing something in each style.

Audience

Whatever <u>type</u> of text you're writing, keep in mind <u>who</u> you're writing for.

Think about who your Audience is

In exam questions, you may only be given vague information — you'll have to decide on the details.

1) <u>Who are you writing for?</u> You'll usually be given some idea of who your audience is:

- <u>A manager of a business</u>. You might be trying to persuade them to employ you, so use formal language to make yourself sound professional.

- <u>A friend</u>. You can be a bit more laid-back with your friends, but don't overdo it.

- <u>Teenagers</u>. You can be fairly informal, but don't go too far — just make sure your writing is interesting for a teenage audience.

- <u>Adults</u>. Be more formal with adults than you would with younger people.

2) Sometimes you won't get much detail about your audience. In this case, write for a <u>general audience</u> — not too technical or too informal.

3) Match the <u>content</u> of your writing to your audience. Choose details that will <u>interest</u> them.

Don't make Informal writing Too Simple

1) If the question asks you to write to a <u>friend</u>, don't write too casually and <u>never</u> use <u>text speak</u>.
2) You can sound <u>chatty</u> but make sure you still include a <u>range</u> of sentences and vocabulary.
3) You can be <u>sarcastic</u> or <u>humorous</u> to make your writing more interesting.

E.g. if you have to write a letter to a friend, this is the sort of thing you <u>should</u> write:

✓ *Of course I'm grateful that they allow me to slave tirelessly into the early hours of the morning.*

But make sure you don't use <u>slang</u> or <u>text speak</u> like this:

✗ *Mate, here's some goss 4 ya. That guy from skool u like stank like 2 much BO 2day.*

You've been a wonderful audience...

If you sent an email to your real friends, your writing would probably be really <u>informal</u>, simple and to the point. But when you write to a 'friend' in the exam, you've got to <u>show off</u> your writing at its <u>very best</u>.

Purpose

<u>Every</u> piece of writing should have a <u>purpose</u> — that means <u>why</u> you're writing it.

Make sure your writing Achieves its Purpose

1) The purpose is your <u>reason</u> for writing. It tells you how your writing should <u>affect</u> your reader.

Some questions have more than one purpose.

2) Purposes (or reasons for writing) are:

Arguing, persuading...	... informing, explaining, advising...	and	describing.
see p.31-36	see p.37-40		see p.41

Exam questions often give you a big hint about the purpose of the piece. E.g.:

> Write a letter to a local business <u>arguing</u> that schools need more support and <u>persuading</u> them to help.

> Write a letter <u>explaining</u> what you do to represent your school at local youth group meetings.

3) Think about the <u>purpose</u> when you're <u>planning</u>. If you're given bullet points, cover <u>all</u> of them.

4) When you've finished writing, <u>read through it</u> and make sure the purpose is <u>clear</u> all the way through.

> E.g. If you're applying for a job, have you <u>informed</u> the reader of your talents, and <u>persuaded</u> them that you're the right person to employ?

Choose the right Language for the purpose

The language you use has to suit your <u>purpose</u>.

1) For example, a letter to the council should be <u>formal</u> and <u>serious</u>...

2) ... but an advert for spot cream aimed at teenagers can be <u>chatty</u> and <u>fun</u>.

3) No matter what you're writing, use a <u>range</u> of vocabulary.

4) Use lots of <u>detail</u> to suit your purpose. E.g. if you're writing to <u>persuade</u>, you could include some <u>shocking statistics</u>. If you're writing to <u>describe</u>, put in details from <u>all five senses</u> (see p.41).

EXAM TIP

Look for the key words in the question...

All the info for which type of text you should write, its purpose and its audience will usually be given in the <u>question</u>. <u>Underline</u> these bits before you start writing to help you <u>focus</u> your answer.

Arguing or Persuading

You need a good <u>argument</u> and truckloads of <u>evidence</u> to persuade your readers to agree with you.

Make sure your writing is **Structured**

1) <u>Work out a plan</u> — spend about five minutes making a plan like the one below.
2) <u>Don't repeat the same idea</u> — use the bullet points (if you're given some) to organise your ideas.
3) <u>Fill in the gaps</u> — once you've planned, try to fit in bits of evidence, facts, examples etc.

Plan your persuasive answers around this **Basic Structure**

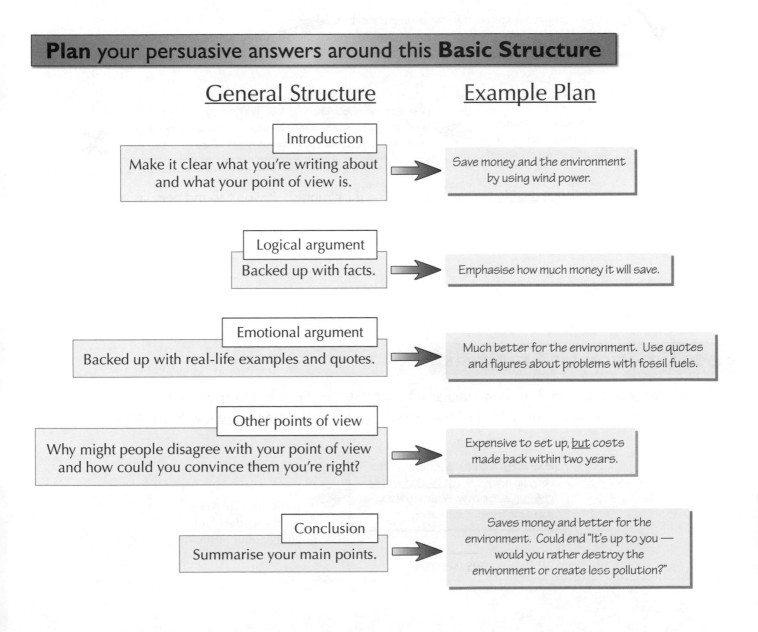

<u>General Structure</u>

<u>Example Plan</u>

Introduction
Make it clear what you're writing about and what your point of view is.
→ Save money and the environment by using wind power.

Logical argument
Backed up with facts.
→ Emphasise how much money it will save.

Emotional argument
Backed up with real-life examples and quotes.
→ Much better for the environment. Use quotes and figures about problems with fossil fuels.

Other points of view
Why might people disagree with your point of view and how could you convince them you're right?
→ Expensive to set up, <u>but</u> costs made back within two years.

Conclusion
Summarise your main points.
→ Saves money and better for the environment. Could end "It's up to you — would you rather destroy the environment or create less pollution?"

I love it when a plan comes together...

<u>Plan</u> what to write, and write what you <u>planned</u>. And remember, if you don't know any facts about the subject you've been asked to write about, you can make them up. Try to make them sound <u>realistic</u> though.

Arguing or Persuading

This page contains a few <u>cunning tricks</u> that you can use to make your writing <u>persuasive</u>.

Use **Reason** to make your argument **Logical**

Your argument must <u>make sense</u>.

1) Show the reader that what you're arguing is the <u>only</u> reasonable <u>point of view</u>.
2) You don't have to <u>agree</u> with what you write. Just make sure you have a <u>strong</u> argument.
3) Use <u>definite</u> language (e.g. 'will', 'all') and sound confident.

> If you're unhappy about the way farm animals are treated, becoming vegetarian isn't the answer. Buying organic meat is a way of supporting farmers who treat their animals well.

Definite language makes answer sound logical.

There's no strong argument here so it sounds more confused.

> Sometimes people who might be worried about the way animals are treated could think it is quite a good idea to become a vegetarian. You could buy organic meat every so often too.

Check your argument is <u>reasonable</u> before you begin — if it's rubbish, it won't sound <u>persuasive</u>.

Add **Emotion** for **Emphasis**

1) Use <u>strong</u> language to show how <u>you feel</u> and to make the reader feel the <u>same way</u>.
2) Don't rely on emotion alone. Start with a sensible argument and <u>emphasise</u> it with emotion.

> If we don't act now, our rivers will be nothing more than <u>dirty sludge</u>. <u>Our children</u> won't know what it's like to paddle in fresh, clear water.

Emotional language makes readers feel <u>guilty</u> about destroying the environment.

Practise writing strong arguments...

To write a really good argument, you need to be logical <u>and</u> use emotion to emphasise your points. Make sure you practise getting both of these things into your writing when you're revising.

Arguing or Persuading

In <u>persuasive</u> writing, make sure you <u>back up</u> your arguments with facts, opinions and examples.

Say if you **Believe** something is **Right or Wrong**

1) Most people share certain beliefs about things that are <u>right and wrong</u>, e.g. 'poverty is bad'.
2) They <u>feel strongly</u> about these things, so it's a <u>good idea</u> to use them in your argument.

> Giving aid to poor nations is not enough, it is by cancelling their debts that we can really make a difference. In many cases debt is crippling their economies, keeping 80% of the population below the poverty line. ✔

You don't actually need to say 'poverty is wrong' — you can assume that your readers will agree with that.

<u>Don't</u> get angry and start <u>ranting</u> in your exam answer and don't write anything that's too <u>over the top</u>.

> Only giving aid to poor nations isn't enough and you'd have to be stupid to disagree. We have to cancel their debt, otherwise we're keeping people poor which is just wrong. ✗

Calm and logical arguments are more likely to <u>convince</u> someone that you're right, rather than just ranting.

Use facts **Carefully**

1) Don't get bogged down in <u>statistics</u>, especially in speeches.
2) Use <u>simple</u>, easy-to-understand facts.
3) This is especially important if you're writing the text for a <u>speech</u> — the people listening will doze off if you go into too much detail.

Confusing — too much detail. →

> Using the Kid800 Wonderpen, 83% of children aged 7 years old wrote an average of 95 words at a speed of 1.58 words per minute. ✗

This is a good statistic, because it's easy to understand. →

> 83% of children could write more quickly when using the Kid800 Wonderpen. ✔

Think about your opinions on common topics...

Have a think about the topics that might come up in the exam — opinions about <u>school</u> and <u>jobs</u> are pretty common ones. If you've already got some ideas ready, it'll <u>save you time</u> in the exam.

Arguing or Persuading

This page tells you about some great ways of <u>backing up</u> your argument.

Use **Opinions** from **Experts**

1) Use expert opinion to <u>back up</u> your arguments.
2) Say <u>who</u> the experts are and <u>how</u> they're related to your argument.
3) You can include expert opinions as <u>quotes</u> (see example below) or explain them in your own words (see p.6).

Don't forget that anything you make up must be <u>realistic</u> — don't claim that <u>100%</u> of people prefer blue to green or quote an <u>expert</u> saying the world is made of soap.

Use **Relevant Quotations**

1) Make sure the quote is <u>relevant</u>.
2) Keep it short. <u>Don't</u> include long extracts.
3) Use <u>quotation marks</u> for direct (exact word) quotations and also say <u>who</u> you're quoting.

> Officer Robert Jones agrees, saying, "I've looked into these recent accidents and I can confirm they were all caused by bad weather."

Use '**Real-life**' Examples

1) Your argument should sound as though it's true in <u>real-life</u>.
2) Give examples that sound realistic to make your argument more <u>convincing</u>.
3) Choose examples that fit your argument as <u>closely</u> as possible.

> After initial concerns, a skate park was built within the main park. Youth crime has since dropped. This was a direct result of the park, according to local police officer Rose Leven. ✓

> The creation of a rose garden in the park has increased visitor numbers. This may have contributed to a reduction in youth crime in the local area. ✗

I know it's true — I made it up myself...

Expert opinions, quotes and real-life examples show the reader that you really <u>know</u> what you're talking about. They also prove to the <u>examiner</u> that you know how to make a really persuasive argument. Sorted.

Arguing or Persuading

Keep your reader's <u>point of view</u> in mind when you write, and grab yourself some juicy marks...

Put yourself in the **Reader's** (or **Listener's**) **Shoes**

1) Any piece of writing will be <u>read</u> or <u>heard</u> by someone — <u>match</u> your writing to your audience.
2) To do this, try to <u>guess</u> what your reader's reactions might be...
3) Your <u>first</u> paragraph is really important — make sure you've got your reader's <u>attention</u> right from the <u>beginning</u>.
4) Show you've thought about the reader's <u>point of view</u>.

Think about what the reader **Cares** about

Think about any <u>concerns</u> the reader might have, and then:

1) Make their concerns sound <u>reasonable</u>.
2) Let them know that you've <u>thought</u> about their concerns.
3) <u>Tell them</u> how your argument addresses their concerns.

> A worry that people may have is the amount of litter after the concert. We will have a team working through the night to clear the area by the next morning.

Imagine how **People** may **Argue Against You**

A good way of persuading people is to imagine how they would argue <u>against you</u>, and answer their points. Imagine you're writing a letter to persuade an animal charity to let you work for them...

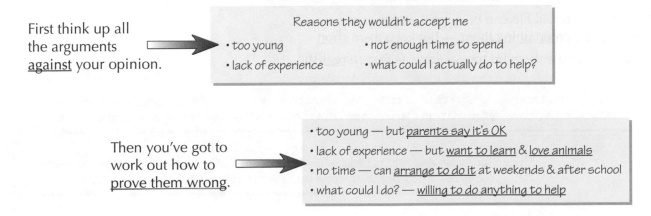

First think up all the arguments <u>against</u> your opinion.

Reasons they wouldn't accept me
- too young
- lack of experience
- not enough time to spend
- what could I actually do to help?

Then you've got to work out how to <u>prove them wrong</u>.

- too young — but <u>parents say it's OK</u>
- lack of experience — but <u>want to learn</u> & <u>love animals</u>
- no time — can <u>arrange to do it</u> at weekends & after school
- what could I do? — <u>willing to do anything to help</u>

Me? Automatically disagree? Absolutely not...

Remember — if you can <u>think</u> like your readers, you'll always be able to stay <u>one step ahead</u> of them. If you can prove their <u>objections</u> wrong even before they've thought of them, then you're onto a <u>winner</u>.

Arguing or Persuading

Writing a really <u>persuasive</u> argument can be hard work — here are some <u>more tips</u> to help you out.

Keep your writing **Polite**

1) Being polite is important when you're writing about people with the <u>opposite opinion</u> to yours.
2) You should criticise their <u>opinions</u> only — don't criticise them personally, or you'll sound angry.

> ✗ A lot of people think school uniforms make everyone equal. They are stupid and wrong...

> ✓ It is often said that school uniforms make everyone equal. This isn't true...

Talk **Directly** to your readers

Use '<u>you</u>' to talk <u>directly</u> to your readers, especially if you're trying to persuade them to do something.

For more on rhetorical questions, see p.42.
For more on rhetorical questions, see p.42.

Using '<u>you</u>' makes the <u>reader</u> feel more <u>involved</u>.

> Giving blood saves lives. As a caring person, do <u>you</u> really need to read further before <u>you</u> take action?

This is a <u>rhetorical question</u>. The reader could only answer it in one way — to say 'no'.

Stories from **Real Life** can be **Entertaining**

1) Stories from real life can be a great way to persuade people by <u>entertaining</u> them — but keep them <u>short</u>.
2) You can make them up too, as long as they're <u>realistic</u>.

> Say you want to persuade parents to let their children cycle to school. Telling a <u>funny story</u> about when you were stuck in a really terrible traffic jam could persuade parents not to drive their kids to school.

> Stories can also be <u>more serious</u>. E.g. if you're persuading a local MP that the pavements in your street are dangerous, you could write about a time when your granny tripped and fell.

REVISION TIP

Get in the habit of using persuasive techniques...

The more you use these techniques, the easier it'll be to include them in your writing. Practise using them as part of your revision until it's all second nature — you'll soon be a persuading pro.

Writing to Inform, Explain or Advise

Non-fiction writing can <u>inform</u>, <u>explain</u> or <u>advise</u> — make sure you know what each one means.

Pick out the **Key Words** in the question

You need a clear idea of your <u>purpose</u> and your <u>audience</u>.
<u>Key words</u> in the question will tell you what the question's asking:

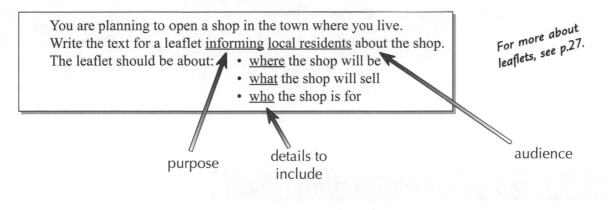

You are planning to open a shop in the town where you live.
Write the text for a leaflet <u>informing</u> <u>local residents</u> about the shop.
The leaflet should be about:
- <u>where</u> the shop will be
- <u>what</u> the shop will sell
- <u>who</u> the shop is for

For more about leaflets, see p.27.

purpose

details to
include

audience

Informing is about **Giving Information** to your reader

Writing to <u>inform</u> means <u>telling</u> your readers about a topic they may not know much about.

1) Informative writing can be <u>practical</u> — e.g. a leaflet giving information about a disease.
2) Or it can be more <u>personal</u> — e.g. a writer informing readers about a time when they ran a marathon.

In either case, you should include plenty of clear <u>facts</u>.

Explaining means helping your readers to **Understand**

When you're explaining, you need to assume your readers <u>don't understand</u> the subject.

1) Give facts, examples and evidence.
2) Decide on the main points you want to make. <u>Explain</u> each point with an example or fact.
3) Tell your readers what any <u>technical terms</u> you use mean — see p.40.

Informing me about informing — too much information...

It's pretty important to know the <u>difference</u> between informing and explaining. <u>Informing</u> is just giving your readers information. <u>Explaining</u> means helping people to understand something they don't at first.

Writing to Inform, Explain or Advise

If you're <u>advising</u> someone, you have to sound like you <u>know</u> what you're talking about.

Advice needs to be based on the Facts

You might have to give <u>advice</u>, e.g. a letter to the council suggesting improvements to a sports centre.

1) Advice should <u>follow on</u> from information you've already written.
2) Keep your advice <u>formal</u> and <u>positive</u>. <u>Don't</u> write things like:

"It's obvious that this should have been done years ago."

This sounds angry and negative

Written advice suggests what Action to take

1) When you're writing to advise, suggest to the reader what <u>courses of action</u> they could take.
2) You could give them different <u>options</u> so they have a <u>choice</u>.
3) Then it's up to the <u>reader</u> to take your advice... or not.

You must tell someone if you're being bullied. This could be:
• your parents
• one of your teachers
• your best friend

Plan your writing carefully

Think about the <u>main things</u> you want to say and note them down in a <u>plan</u>.
Here's an example of a "writing to inform" question:

Write the text for an information leaflet about your school or college for potential students and their parents.

If the question includes bullet points, use these to plan your essay.

And here's a plan of the <u>main points</u> you might mention in your answer:

<u>Purpose</u>: to inform   <u>Form</u>: leaflet   <u>Audience</u>: potential students and their parents.

<u>Points to include</u>:
1) Big school — 1500 pupils.   2) Loads of choice of <u>subjects</u>.   3) Students get <u>good grades</u>.

Read the question, plan your answer, write it and check it...

Planning your writing is really <u>useful</u>. It'll help you to answer the <u>question</u> and get lots of lovely <u>marks</u>.
If you make a great plan, it'll also <u>stop</u> you from panicking in the middle of the exam. Excellent stuff.

Writing to Inform, Explain or Advise

Always remember <u>why</u> you're writing your text — for more on <u>purpose</u>, see p.30.

Layout can help you Organise your writing

If you're writing a <u>leaflet</u>, you can use <u>headings</u> and <u>bullet points</u> to organise the text:

> 1) <u>Headings</u> break text up into <u>sections</u> and tell the reader what that section is <u>about</u>.
> 2) <u>Bullet points</u> are a good way to split information into lists of <u>facts</u>.

<u>Only</u> use these methods if it makes sense. E.g. headings work well in a newspaper article, bullet points work well in a leaflet. Otherwise, <u>write in paragraphs</u>.

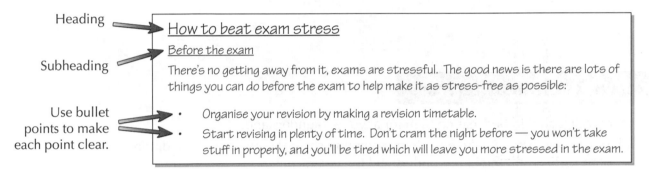

Heading

Subheading

Use bullet points to make each point clear.

<u>How to beat exam stress</u>

<u>Before the exam</u>

There's no getting away from it, exams are stressful. The good news is there are lots of things you can do before the exam to help make it as stress-free as possible:

- Organise your revision by making a revision timetable.
- Start revising in plenty of time. Don't cram the night before — you won't take stuff in properly, and you'll be tired which will leave you more stressed in the exam.

Using "I" or "You" can sound too personal

If you use "I..." a lot, it can sound as if you're just expressing <u>your opinion</u>.
That's fine for some pieces but it can make information or advice sound <u>unconvincing</u>.

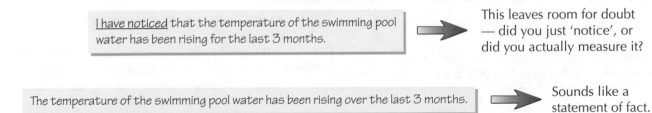

<u>I have noticed</u> that the temperature of the swimming pool water has been rising for the last 3 months.

This leaves room for doubt — did you just 'notice', or did you actually measure it?

The temperature of the swimming pool water has been rising over the last 3 months.

Sounds like a statement of fact.

Using "I..." can be handy if you're writing about your <u>own</u> experience. Just don't use it all the time.

EXAM TIP

Pay attention to the form you're writing in...

Using <u>headings</u> and <u>bullet points</u> can help to give your writing a really clear <u>structure</u>, but you should only use them in the exam if they're <u>suitable</u> for the form you've been asked to write in.

Writing to Inform, Explain or Advise

You've got to make sure <u>everyone</u> knows what you're on about when you write to inform, explain or advise.

Think about your **Readers**

If you're writing to <u>inform</u> or <u>explain</u>, don't assume your readers will know everything about the topic.

1) Explain things which might be obvious to you, but not to <u>other people</u>.

This is no good —

> Get a plant and grow it.

You need to explain what you mean —

> Buy some seeds from a garden centre. Dig a small hole and put the seeds in the hole. Water the area regularly.

2) Guess where the reader might get confused and make those bits especially <u>clear</u>.

Explain **Technical** terms...

1) Your writing should be clear enough for anyone to <u>understand</u>.

2) Take care even when you're explaining something as <u>ordinary</u> as cooking dinner — some readers still might not understand the technical terms you're using.

The underlined words are <u>technical terms</u>. They'll be understood by tennis fans...

> The <u>serve and volley</u> game of Jones dominated Smith's <u>groundstrokes</u>.

...but others may not understand, and get confused.

...but don't make your language **Too Simple**

1) If you don't use the right words, it might seem like you don't know what you're talking about....

> There are several different types of singer. Some singers sound really squeaky when they sing, and some singers don't.

This is all pretty obvious — it would be better if the writer had <u>named</u> and <u>explained</u> the different types of voice (soprano, baritone etc.).

2) ... and sometimes it might be <u>unclear</u> what you mean.

> I have spoken to <u>many people</u> and <u>many of them</u> are concerned about graffiti.

'Many' is vague — be <u>more specific</u> and explain <u>how many</u> people and <u>who</u> they are (students, parents etc.).

Assume the reader won't understand technical words...

<u>Technical jargon</u> can often be confusing, so it's <u>important</u> to explain any technical words you use. <u>Imagine</u> the examiner doesn't understand technical language and you have to <u>explain</u> it to them.

Writing to Describe

A <u>great</u> piece of descriptive writing will really bring a scene to <u>life</u> in the reader's mind.

You're painting a **Picture** with **Words**

1) When you're <u>writing to describe</u>, remember that the <u>reader</u> won't have the same <u>picture</u> in their head as you have in yours — you need to <u>draw it</u> for them with words.
2) Come up with <u>creative</u> ways to describe what you're thinking about.
3) You can use your <u>own experiences</u> — but remember you can add in <u>invented details</u> too.

Imagine you're making a **Film** of the scene

Imagine that you're making a <u>film</u> of your scene, and you're describing what will happen in it.

1) Think about how the scene will <u>look</u> at <u>different times</u> of the day, or in <u>different seasons</u>.

> The beach was lonely and grey, empty of all movement except the soft splash of waves. It was hard to believe that it would soon be alive with tourists and brightly-coloured deck chairs.

2) Or you could <u>zoom</u> in or out of your scene, <u>describing things</u> as you go.

> I was only feet away from the last of the day's fishermen looking out to sea. The reflections of trees shimmered on the water, and in the distance I could just make out the hazy form of hills.

Think about each of the **Senses** when you write

You can't use every single one all the time, but the senses can be used to make a scene <u>come to life</u>.

Sight — How things looked...

The wall crumbled away to reveal a small tunnel winding into the distance.

Sound — How things sounded...

There was a loud roaring from the crowd by the stage.

Smell — How things smelled...

The pleasant smell of freshly-baked bread hung in the air.

Taste — How things tasted...

The soup tasted salty and contained lots of chewy lumps.

Touch — How things felt...

I felt the sharp crunch of rocks and stones under my feet as I walked along towards the sea.

The reader needs to be able to imagine what you're writing about...

OK so all this 'paint a picture with words' stuff might sound weird, but it's the best way to get this right. When you're writing, make sure you use a <u>broad range</u> of language and describe things using the <u>senses</u>.

Useful Language for Non-Fiction Texts

Here are some extra tips to make your writing even more amazing. Read carefully and practise.

Use Rhetorical Questions to Involve your audience

A rhetorical question doesn't need an answer — the answer should be obvious from the text.

Is this sort of thing acceptable in our society?

Letting readers come up with the answer themselves is a great way to make them agree with you.

Can anyone tell me why road builders are ruining the countryside?

Use emotional language (like "ruining the countryside") to emphasise your feelings on the subject.

Use Lists of Three

It's one of the easiest and most useful tricks for emphasising your points.
Instead of just using one adjective in a sentence, use three.

Making children sit more exams would be stressful, time-consuming and unreasonable.

This sounds much better than "More exams would be stressful and time-consuming".

Be Careful when you're using Exaggeration

1) Sometimes you can use an exaggeration in your writing to make your point sound stronger.

These days, teachers have to wade through tonnes of paperwork every week.

Your readers will realise you don't literally mean tonnes. It just stresses that you're talking about a lot of paperwork.

2) Use exaggeration carefully. If it's not obvious to the reader that you're exaggerating, they might think you're just a bit confused.

This exaggeration is the best thing ever...

The techniques on this page can be very powerful, but if you use them too much your answer will start to sound too wordy and confusing. Get them into your answer, but use them carefully and don't overdo it.

Warm-Up Questions

Writing non-fiction texts isn't always a piece of cake, but if you've read through this section, you should be able to do these warm-up questions. After that, you can try some practice exam questions (they're just like the real deal). The Foundation level questions are on page 44, and the Higher level ones are on page 46. For more excitement, there's a worked exam answer to one question from each level too — these are on pages 45 and 47-48.

Warm-Up Questions

1) Write the first paragraph of a letter to your local MP arguing against the closure of the youth centre near your house.

2) Imagine you're writing for a TV guide. Write a short review of the worst programme you've seen this week.

3) You're giving a speech at your school tomorrow to encourage people to vote for you as class representative. Write a summary of what you're going to say which you could use as the introduction to your speech.

4) You're on holiday with your grandparents. Write a postcard to your best friend, letting them know what you've been up to and what you're looking forward to.

5) You've been selected for the school's debating team. Write three key ideas for an argument that will persuade people to make more use of public transport.

6) Underline the bits where the writer adds emotion to their argument:

> Dear Mum — Just thought I should write a little note to explain why I'd really like to get a dog. I'm not just thinking of myself because you would be able to take the dog for walks as well as me. This means you'd get some exercise every day, and it's cheaper than gym membership. This would save money that could be spent on the dog's food and vet bills. You see? It all evens out. Also, everyone else has a pet and I've wanted a pet dog for so long, and I feel left out. And there are so many dogs out there that just need a good home... like ours? Love Darren

7) Which is more likely to persuade your reader — a balanced argument or a ranting one?

8) Make up quotes from experts that could be used to support the following arguments:
   a) Spending more than 2 hours a day on the internet could affect your eyesight.
   b) It's important to eat at least five pieces of fruit and vegetables a day.
   c) Chewing gum should be banned in all schools.

9) Write a few sentences for a leaflet explaining your favourite hobby or a sport to a reader who knows nothing about it. Remember to explain any technical terms.

10) Which of these is the less interesting and less vivid description? Why?
   a) He wore a long, black overcoat that was ragged at the edges and fading in colour. His tattered hat was tilted to cover his eyes. As he loomed over me, I felt my heart in my mouth. I couldn't breathe.
   b) He wore an old coat and when he came near me, I was scared.

11) Rewrite the statements below as rhetorical questions. The first has been done for you.
   a) Eating chocolate every day reduces stress levels.
      Who'd have thought that eating chocolate every day could reduce stress levels?
   b) To everyone's surprise, Mikey was spotted on a date with Laura.
   c) I wish people wouldn't talk in the library.

Exam Questions

Try these Foundation exam practice questions and polish your writing skills till they're sparkling. Check out the worked answer to a similar question on p.45 for some extra inspiration.

1. Write a letter to a friend telling them about your most memorable birthday celebration. The letter should include:

   • Where and when the birthday celebration took place

   • Why the birthday celebration was memorable for you

   • Anything else that made the birthday celebration interesting.

   (16 marks)

2. Write a talk for your year assembly about some work experience that you've done recently. The talk should include:

   • Information about the work experience and where it took place

   • How you got the work experience

   • What you learnt from the work experience.

   (16 marks)

3. Write an article for your school newspaper, persuading students to do a sponsored walk for charity. The article should include:

   • Some details about the walk and where it will be held

   • Reasons why people should take part in the walk

   • Which charity the walk is raising money for and why it is important.

   (24 marks)

4. Write a letter to the board of governors at your school arguing for or against free musical instrument lessons for all students. The letter should be about:

   • Whether you are for or against the lessons and why

   • What the good or bad effects of the lessons might be

   • Whether parents and students would support your argument.

   (24 marks)

Worked Exam Answer FOUNDATION

To get the gist of these non-fiction writing exam questions, here's an example answer — with plenty of ideas for writing a really cracking text.

---

1. Places can seem different at different times of year. Choose a place and write a letter to a friend telling them what that place is like in winter and in summer. The letter should include:

   - What the place is like in winter

   - How it's different in summer

   - Whether you prefer the place in winter or in summer.

   (16 marks)

Essay plan

1) Begin by describing the country lane in winter — concentrate on the feelings of cold.
2) Describe the harshness of the landscape and the trees struggling to survive.
3) Describe the country lane in summer — contrasting the beauty of the landscape with that of winter.
4) Describe the wildlife and all of nature coming to life again.

Written in the form of a letter

Dear Sameer,

Describes touch

    I'm so glad you're coming to visit in summer. East Ibley in winter is horrible! I went for a walk along the lane today and the rain was freezing, like little bits of glass hitting me. The leaves were a dull brown mush that squelched underfoot and clung to my boots. The poplar trees, usually so tall and leafy, were ruined by the winter's cold, and each branch was empty and barren. The undergrowth around the trees appeared dark and gloomy, as if it held dark secrets. The whole scene was grey, as if life had been sucked from it.

Dramatic images

    The clouds looked like monstrous faces, as if nature was angry at the world. The branches from a fallen tree, blown over the night before, were scattered across the lane like litter. The rain was forming muddy pools and filling potholes.

Suggests how the scene makes her feel

Compares with the details of the place in winter

    But when you visit, it will be lovely. The poplar trees will be leafy again, and swaying gently in the summer breeze. We'll wander along, clutching ice creams and smelling of sun cream. I can't wait!

    The sun's rays will be warm and gentle, and the sky will be a deep, deep blue at that time of year. There are so many flowers here in summer: proud, tall foxgloves and delicate red poppies and bright white daisies popping up amongst the lush green grass. Maybe we'll see butterflies, with white wings, flitting around in the haze of heat. There will be birds singing to each other, and lots of new life everywhere. The summer here is so much nicer than the winter — I can't wait!

Lots of objects and colours to describe the scene

I hope you're looking forward to the visit as much as I am.
Love Beth

Exam Questions

Make sure you're fully prepared for the exam by having a go at these Higher practice questions.
Look at the worked exam answer on pages 47-48 for more ideas on writing non-fiction texts.

Section Three — Writing Non-Fiction Texts

1. Write a letter to a friend describing a recent trip or holiday.

   (16 marks)

2. Imagine that you are the chairman of a national charity. Write the text for a talk explaining what your charity does and informing people what they can do to help.

   (16 marks)

3. Write an article for a teen magazine, in which you argue that the age of voting should be lowered to 16.

   (24 marks)

Worked Exam Answer

On these two pages, there's a worked exam answer to a Higher non-fiction writing question. Give it a read — there are lots of tips on how to tackle these questions and make your writing really top-notch.

1. Write the text for a leaflet encouraging young people to undertake work experience.

(16 marks)

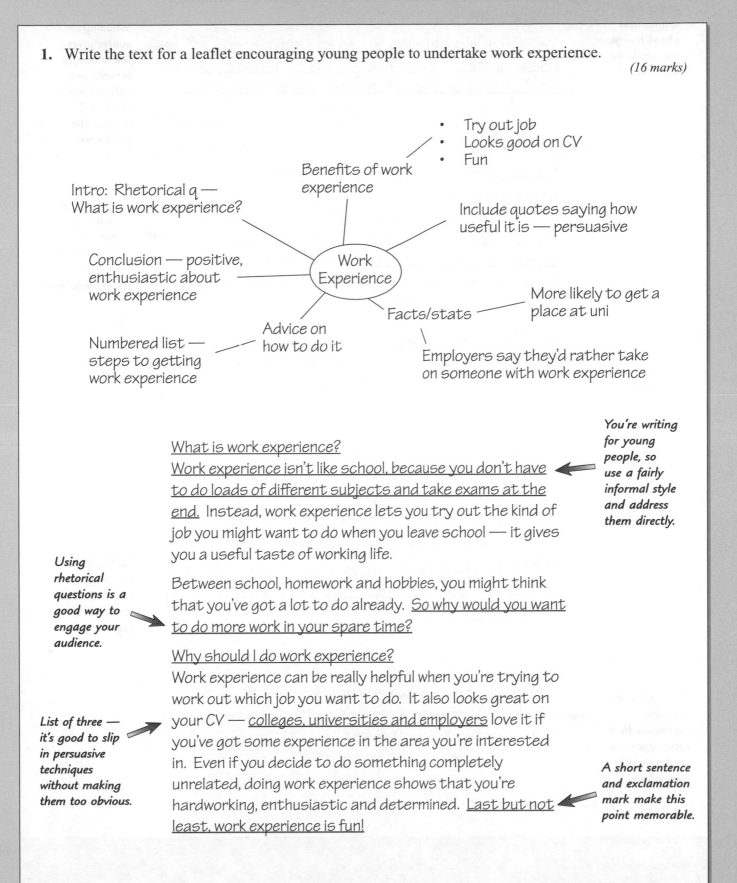

- Try out job
- Looks good on CV
- Fun

Benefits of work experience

Intro: Rhetorical q — What is work experience?

Include quotes saying how useful it is — persuasive

Conclusion — positive, enthusiastic about work experience

Work Experience

More likely to get a place at uni

Numbered list — steps to getting work experience

Advice on how to do it

Facts/stats

Employers say they'd rather take on someone with work experience

---

<u>What is work experience?</u>
<u>Work experience isn't like school, because you don't have to do loads of different subjects and take exams at the end.</u> Instead, work experience lets you try out the kind of job you might want to do when you leave school — it gives you a useful taste of working life.

You're writing for young people, so use a fairly informal style and address them directly.

Between school, homework and hobbies, you might think that you've got a lot to do already. <u>So why would you want to do more work in your spare time?</u>

Using rhetorical questions is a good way to engage your audience.

<u>Why should I do work experience?</u>
Work experience can be really helpful when you're trying to work out which job you want to do. It also looks great on your CV — <u>colleges, universities and employers</u> love it if you've got some experience in the area you're interested in. Even if you decide to do something completely unrelated, doing work experience shows that you're hardworking, enthusiastic and determined. <u>Last but not least, work experience is fun!</u>

List of three — it's good to slip in persuasive techniques without making them too obvious.

A short sentence and exclamation mark make this point memorable.

Worked Exam Answer

It's good to give a few suggestions about how your text could be laid out.

[Quote in a separate text box with a photo of a smiling girl holding a cat]

"I've always loved animals, so I did work experience in an animal shelter. The work has been really interesting, and now I know for sure what I want to do when I leave school."

— Kayley, 15

Including quotes gives you a chance to write in a different style, which will impress the examiners.

Sounds good... but will it help me get a job?
Whether you're thinking of getting a job straight from school, or going to uni, work experience will help you. Students who do work experience are more likely to be offered a place at their first choice university, and 70% of employers say they'd rather hire someone who'd done some work experience.

Making up facts and statistics is a great way to sound knowledgeable.

I'm in! What do I do next?

Numbered lists can make your text easier to remember, especially if you're giving advice.

1) The first step is to decide where you'd like to do work experience. For example if you've always wanted to be a nurse, do work experience in a hospital. If you're not really sure what you want to do, have a think about what your interests are — for example, if you love swimming, you could try being a lifeguard.

2) Write a letter applying for the work experience. You need to explain why you want to do work experience there and what you can offer (your skills and abilities).

3) Not all companies are set up to take on work experience people, so don't worry if you get rejected — just try another one.

Addressing the reader's concerns helps to support your argument.

Conclusion

Finish off with a positive conclusion that encourages the reader to follow your advice.

Remember, your work experience now could make all the difference in your future career, so get out there and start applying. You won't regret it!

Revision Summary

This section covers the <u>main forms of texts</u> you might have to write in the exam, but <u>don't panic</u> if you get something different — the basic advice is still the same. Just think about your <u>audience</u> and your <u>purpose</u>. To check you've got the hang of it, here are a few questions to test your knowledge.

Different Forms (p27-28) ☑

1) How should your style of writing be different in a formal and an informal letter?
2) Name two techniques you could use in a newspaper article to make it easier to read.
3) If you're writing a film review, why is it important to include some facts about the film itself?
4) What's the main difference between a speech and other types of non-fiction text?

Audience (p29) ☑

5) Give three examples of audiences you might write for. Say whether you would write in a formal or informal way for each one.

Purpose (p30) ☑

6) What is meant by the 'purpose' of your writing?

Arguing or Persuading (p31-36) ☑

7) Put these points of a plan for a persuasive answer into the correct order:
Emotional argument, Introduction, Logical argument, Conclusion, Other points of view.
8) Why might the sentence "Everyone deserves an education" help get the reader on your side?
9) Which of these quotes would be appropriate in an essay on getting good grades, and why?
a) "Exams changed my entire existence", said a stranger in the street.
b) "My GCSE grades have helped me to achieve my goals", said the Prime Minister.
10) Do all the facts and opinions you use in non-fiction answers have to come from real sources?
11) Why should you address any concerns you think your reader might have about your argument?
12) Explain why you need to keep your writing style polite.
13) Give one reason why you might include a story from real life in your writing.

Writing to Inform, Explain or Advise (p37-40) ☑

14) What's the main difference between writing to inform and writing to explain?
15) True or false: when writing to advise, you should suggest what action the reader could take?
16) Why should you explain any technical terms you use in your writing?

Writing to Describe (p41) ☑

17) a) Give a short example of an interesting and a boring description of someone's face.
b) Explain why one is better than the other.
18) Choose two of the five senses and give an example of how each might be used to describe your local area to a visitor.

Useful Language for Non-Fiction Texts (p42) ☑

19) What is a rhetorical question and why are rhetorical questions effective?
20) Why should you be careful when using exaggeration in your writing?

Make Your Writing Clear to Read

A <u>big chunk</u> of the marks for a writing exam question are for <u>how</u> you write, not what you write about.

Writing **Well** gets you a better grade

This is what you'll be marked on:

1) <u>Standard English</u> (see p.51)
   Examiners will expect you to use Standard English.
   Don't slip into slang or local dialect, or you'll lose marks.

2) <u>Punctuation</u> (see p.52-54)
   Punctuation is brilliant for making your writing smooth, clear and punchy —
   but only if you get it right. Make sure you know when to use commas, apostrophes etc.

3) <u>Spelling and types of words</u> (see p.57-59)
   Your spelling needs to be pretty accurate if you want a good grade,
   and it also helps if you know how to use different types of words correctly.

4) <u>Sentence types</u> (see p.60)
   Use a mixture of sentence structures — from short and simple to long and complex.

5) <u>Using varied language</u> (see p.61-62)
   Use similes and metaphors when you're describing something,
   and make sure you use some interesting words too.

6) <u>Paragraphs</u> (see p.4)
   Writing in paragraphs is very important for organising your writing into manageable sections.

Writing bad English don't get you nowhere...

If you learn the <u>rules</u> in this section and remember to use them when you're writing, you won't go too far wrong. Make sure you <u>check</u> your work before you hand it in, so you can correct any <u>obvious</u> mistakes.

Standard English

The <u>examiners</u> want you to use <u>Standard English</u>, so you'll lose marks if you don't know how...

Use **Standard English**

1) People in different areas use <u>different local words</u> (dialect) that can be hard for others to understand.
2) <u>Standard English</u> avoids any dialect words and is understood by people all over the country.

Using Standard English means following some **Simple Rules**

1) Don't write the <u>informal words</u> you'd say when talking to your friends, e.g. 'OK', 'yeah'.
2) <u>Don't</u> use <u>slang</u>, local <u>dialect words</u> or <u>text speak</u>.
3) Use <u>correct</u> spelling and grammar.

Avoid these **Common Mistakes**

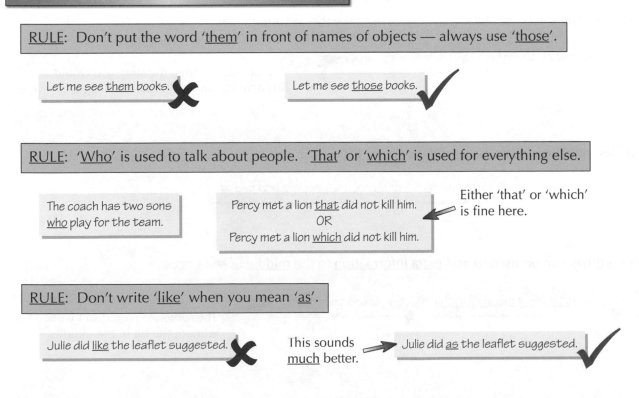

<u>RULE</u>: Don't put the word '<u>them</u>' in front of names of objects — always use '<u>those</u>'.

Let me see <u>them</u> books. ✗   Let me see <u>those</u> books. ✓

<u>RULE</u>: '<u>Who</u>' is used to talk about people. '<u>That</u>' or '<u>which</u>' is used for everything else.

The coach has two sons <u>who</u> play for the team.

Percy met a lion <u>that</u> did not kill him.
OR
Percy met a lion <u>which</u> did not kill him.

Either 'that' or 'which' is fine here.

<u>RULE</u>: Don't write '<u>like</u>' when you mean '<u>as</u>'.

Julie did <u>like</u> the leaflet suggested. ✗   This sounds <u>much</u> better. → Julie did <u>as</u> the leaflet suggested. ✓

You should try to use Standard English in the exam...

EXAM TIP: The only time you might use <u>non-standard English</u> in the exam is if you're quoting someone else's <u>speech</u> (and that's how they speak). Most of the time you should stick to using <u>Standard English</u>.

Punctuation

Punctuation isn't just there to make your essays look <u>pretty</u> — it makes your writing a lot <u>clearer</u>.

Start and Finish your sentences correctly

Always <u>start</u> sentences with a <u>capital letter</u>. Sentences always <u>end</u> with either:

1) a full stop — use these for most sentences. ➡ •

2) a question mark — use these if the sentence is asking a question. ➡ ?

3) an exclamation mark — use these if you want your sentence to have a strong impact. ➡ !

You should never use exclamation marks in your answers to reading questions — and try not to overuse them in the writing section either.

Use Commas to put Pauses in sentences

1) Commas <u>separate</u> the parts of long sentences to make the meaning clear.

> In the valley below, the villages all seemed very small.

Without the comma, the sentence would begin 'in the valley below the villages'.

2) Commas are also used to break up the items in a <u>list</u>:

> I bought onions, mushrooms, peppers and pasta.

3) <u>Pairs of commas</u> can be used to add <u>extra information</u> to the <u>middle</u> of sentences:

> Elijah, <u>who was raising money for charity</u>, completed the course.

comma   comma

The sentence would still work without the bit in the middle.

You need to learn this stuff on punctuation — full stop...

It's really <u>difficult</u> to read a text which has no punctuation at all, so you've got to make sure you use it in the exam. When you've finished your writing, <u>check</u> it to make sure there aren't any <u>silly</u> mistakes in it.

Apostrophes

Apostrophes can seem <u>tricky</u>, but they're not actually too difficult if you stick to a few <u>simple rules</u>...

Add 's to show **Who Owns** something

The horse belongs to Abby so you add an <u>apostrophe</u> + '<u>s</u>' to the name of the owner.

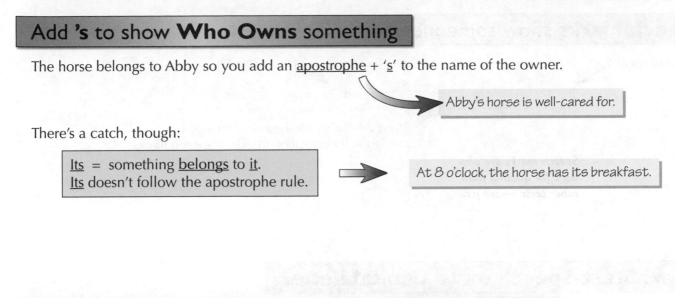

Abby's horse is well-cared for.

There's a catch, though:

<u>Its</u> = something <u>belongs</u> to <u>it</u>.
<u>Its</u> doesn't follow the apostrophe rule.

At 8 o'clock, the horse has its breakfast.

It gets a bit **Tricky** with **Groups of People** or **Things**

The <u>foxes'</u> den was found during the <u>men's</u> cross-country race.

1) If it already ends in <u>s</u>, stick an apostrophe on the <u>end</u> but <u>not</u> an extra <u>s</u>.

2) Plural words that don't end in s, e.g. <u>men</u> and <u>mice</u>, follow the normal rule of apostrophe + 's'.

Apostrophes can show where there's a **Missing Letter**

1) You can <u>shorten</u> some pairs of words by sticking them together and cutting out letters.
2) You put an <u>apostrophe</u> to show where you've removed the letters from.

E.g. I am ➡ I'm

The letter 'a' has been removed, so an apostrophe goes <u>in its place</u>.

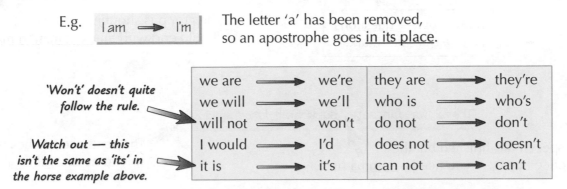

'Won't' doesn't quite follow the rule.

Watch out — this isn't the same as 'its' in the horse example above.

we are ➡ we're		they are ➡ they're
we will ➡ we'll		who is ➡ who's
will not ➡ won't		do not ➡ don't
I would ➡ I'd		does not ➡ doesn't
it is ➡ it's		can not ➡ can't

Impress the examiner — use apostrophes properly...

And now, a quick word of <u>warning</u> — never, <u>ever</u> use an apostrophe to show that something's <u>plural</u> (for example: two banana's, five pear's). I know your greengrocer might do it, but that doesn't make it right.

Speech Marks

You guessed it — speech marks are yet another thing the examiner will be <u>looking out for</u>.

Speech Marks show someone's Actually Speaking

Start of speech

End of speech

"Protecting the environment is important," said the volunteer.

These are the words the volunteer said — they go in the <u>quotation marks</u>, or <u>speech marks</u>.

Speech marks are also used for quoting from other texts — see p.6.

Always Start Speech with a Capital Letter

"My inspiration is my grandfather, an inventor," Louise told me.

Here's the <u>capital letter</u>.

The speech bit <u>always</u> begins with a capital letter — even if it isn't at the start of the sentence.

I asked Louise, "Why is your design special?"

"My invention," Louise explained, "will help elderly people."

If speech is <u>broken up</u>, the second part <u>doesn't need a capital letter</u> (unless you're starting a new sentence).

End speech with a Question Mark, Full Stop or Comma

"If the youth club shuts, where will our kids go?" asked one parent.

Remember — <u>questions</u> need a question mark.

The group shouted, "Come and join us!"

The group is shouting, so this should end with an <u>exclamation mark</u>.

"The fair was fantastic," said Sarah Jones, aged 24.

The speech has finished but the sentence hasn't — you need a <u>comma</u> here.

The sentence finishes here, so you need a <u>full stop</u>.

Learn these rules for using speech marks...

REVISION TIP

It's not enough to just learn where the <u>speech marks</u> go in your writing — you need to know how to punctuate the <u>rest</u> of the speech too. Try practising by writing out a <u>conversation</u> with a friend.

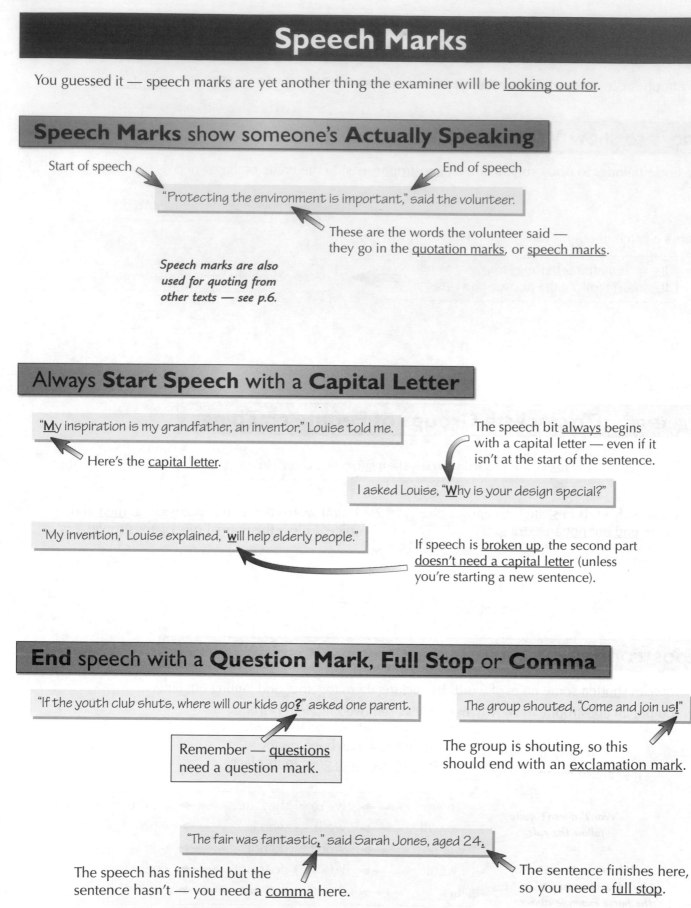

Negatives

It's a page about <u>negatives</u> — deep breath, chin up and don't let it get you down.

'No' Isn't the only Negative word

The easiest way to make a phrase negative is to add '<u>no</u>' or '<u>not</u>' (or by adding <u>-n't</u> to a word, see p.53).

Positive sentence: | My aubergines are rotten.

Negative sentence: | My aubergines are <u>not</u> rotten.

Don't use Double Negatives

<u>Two negative words</u> in the same phrase will make it <u>positive</u>, e.g.:

I <u>don't</u> want <u>no</u> aubergine.　　　REALLY MEANS　　　I <u>do</u> want some aubergine.

Only use <u>one negative</u> at a time. ➡ I <u>don't</u> want any aubergine.

The word None has different meanings

1) '<u>None</u>' can cause problems, because it has different meanings.

It can mean 'not one': | <u>None</u> of the students passed the test.

It can also mean 'not any': | I want an aubergine, but there are <u>none</u> left.

2) The main thing you need to remember is that 'none' should <u>not</u> be used with other negative words:

He has <u>not got none</u>. ✗　　　　　He has <u>none</u>. ✓

Stop being so negative — it's not that bad...

Negative sentences can be very <u>useful</u> in your writing and can make it sound more <u>interesting</u>, as long as they're used correctly. Remember the points on this page to collect some <u>positive</u> marks in your exams.

Warm-Up Questions

You could work through this page in a flash, but there's no point unless you check over any bits you don't know and make sure you understand everything. It's not quick, but it's the only way.

Warm-Up Questions

1) Which of these should you check for when you finish a piece of writing?
   a) correct punctuation
   b) cauliflowers
   c) paragraphs properly divided up
   d) spelling all right
   e) bookworms

2) What is 'Standard English'?

3) Do you need to use Standard English in your GCSE exam?

4) Can you think of any parts of your English GCSE when it would be all right <u>not</u> to use Standard English?

5) Choose the grammatically correct sentence in each of the following pairs:
   a) *Give me them pens.*
      or *Give me those pens.*
   b) *A barrister is a lawyer who speaks in court.*
      or *A barrister is a lawyer which speaks in court.*
   c) *The boy did as the teacher said.*
      or *The boy did like the teacher said.*

6) What do you <u>always</u> have to have at the beginning of a sentence?

7) What are the three things you can use to finish your sentence?

8) Write down three ways you can use a comma.

9) Write out these sentences with the correct punctuation:
   a) the man who still hadnt recovered from his cold was feeling ill
   b) i need to buy chicken cherries chocolate cheese and chips
   c) why wont Roberts dog play with the childrens dog
   d) Sarah asked has anyone seen Liz today
   e) does anyone want another cup of tea Andy asked because Im having one

10) Write out these sentences and add in the apostrophes you need.
   a) Charlies dogs were eating bananas.
   b) I dont like Franks new trousers.
   c) Mum says its going to rain today.

11) What will the examiners think you mean if you write 'I don't want to do no English exam'?

Spelling

Some spelling mistakes are really <u>common</u> — luckily this page tells you how to <u>avoid</u> making them.

Don't confuse **Different** words that **Sound** the **Same**

Two words that sound similar can mean different things. Here are some common examples to look out for:

1) affect / effect

1) <u>Affect</u> means 'to influence something'. ➡ Burning fossil fuels <u>affects</u> the Earth's climate.
2) An <u>effect</u> is the result of an action. ➡ The <u>effect</u> of burning fossil fuels is global warming.

2) there / their / they're

1) <u>There</u> is used to talk about <u>place</u>. ➡ The accident happened over <u>there</u>.
2) <u>Their</u> shows that someone <u>owns</u> something. ➡ <u>Their</u> clothes were stylish.
3) <u>They're</u> is the short form of '<u>they are</u>'. ➡ <u>They're</u> the top competitors.

3) where / were / wear

1) <u>Where</u> is used to talk about <u>place</u>. ➡ <u>Where</u> else can young people go for support?
2) <u>Were</u> is the past tense of the verb '<u>to be</u>'. ➡ They <u>were</u> collected by bus.
3) <u>Wear</u> is what you do with clothes, shoes etc. ➡ Students must <u>wear</u> their uniforms.

4) your / you're

1) <u>Your</u> means something that belongs to <u>you</u>. ➡ Please give me <u>your</u> support!
2) <u>You're</u> is the short form of '<u>you are</u>'. ➡ <u>You're</u> only allowed one vote.

Watch out for these **Common Spelling Mistakes**

1) Words with a <u>silent 'h'</u> — you don't say it, but you must write it: e.g. c<u>h</u>emistry.
2) Words written with '<u>ph</u>' and pronounced with an 'f' sound: e.g. gra<u>ph</u> or <u>ph</u>iloso<u>ph</u>y.
3) Words with an '<u>i' before an 'e</u>' except <u>after 'c</u>': e.g. rel<u>ie</u>f or rec<u>ei</u>ve
4) Words where the <u>endings change</u> when they're made <u>plural</u>: e.g. bab<u>ies</u> not bab<u>ys</u>.

Correct (~~yor~~ your) spelling errors neatly...

If you do make a spelling mistake, you can correct it neatly by putting brackets around the word, putting two lines through it and writing the correction above. See p.8 for more on correcting errors.

Nouns, Verbs, Adverbs and Adjectives

You need to know the proper <u>names</u> for the different <u>types</u> of words, so get your learning hat on.

A **Noun** is a **Person, Place** or **Thing**

There are four kinds of noun:

1) '<u>Proper</u>' names (towns, people, months etc.), e.g. Gloria, Sunday, Texas.
2) <u>Groups</u> of people or things, e.g. class, pack, squad.
3) <u>Names</u> of other <u>everyday things</u>, e.g. hedge, hair, woman.
4) Words for <u>ideas</u>, e.g. truth, beauty, fear.

Proper names always have <u>capital letters</u>.

Verbs are '**Doing**' or '**Being**' words

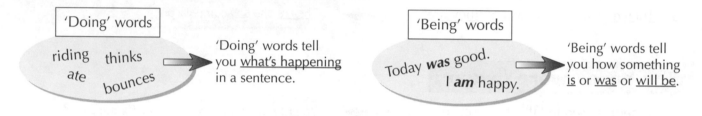

'Doing' words

riding thinks
ate bounces

'Doing' words tell you <u>what's happening</u> in a sentence.

'Being' words

Today **was** good.
I **am** happy.

'Being' words tell you how something <u>is</u> or <u>was</u> or <u>will be</u>.

Adjectives describe **Things** and **People**

Global warming is <u>bad</u>. ✗

Too boring — <u>zero marks alert</u>!

Global warming is a <u>serious</u> and <u>worrying</u> issue. ✓

Much better — the <u>adjectives</u> will impress the examiner.

Adverbs describe **How** an **Action** is done

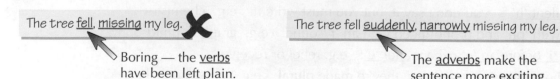

The tree <u>fell</u>, <u>missing</u> my leg. ✗

Boring — the <u>verbs</u> have been left plain.

The tree fell <u>suddenly</u>, <u>narrowly</u> missing my leg. ✓

The <u>adverbs</u> make the sentence more <u>exciting</u>.

Variety is the spice of English essays...

Use lots of different <u>verbs</u>, <u>adjectives</u> and <u>adverbs</u> in your writing and don't repeat the same word too often. This will make your writing more <u>interesting</u> to read, and bag you loads of marks from the examiner.

Using Verbs in Sentences

The message of this page is that your sentences need to <u>make sense</u>. Simple, but very important.

Verbs can have different Tenses

1) Verbs are '<u>doing</u>' words or '<u>being</u>' words (see p.58).
2) The form of the verb <u>changes</u> depending on <u>when</u> the action takes place.

In the past:

> Mr Smith <u>was</u> the show's first performer.

In the future:

> Mr Smith <u>will be</u> the show's first performer.

These are both '<u>being</u>' words — but they're in different tenses.

Make sure you use the Right Form of the verb

1) Every <u>verb</u> describes what someone (or something) is <u>doing</u> (or <u>being</u>).
2) If there's only <u>one person</u> doing something, use the <u>singular</u> form of the verb.
3) If there's <u>more than one person</u> doing something, use the <u>plural</u> form of the verb.
4) When you're writing a verb in a sentence, say it <u>out loud</u>. Decide whether it <u>sounds right</u> or not.

> They <u>was</u> eating cheese sandwiches. ✗

This sounds wrong. '<u>They</u>' means more than one person, so the subject is <u>plural</u>.

> They <u>were</u> eating cheese sandwiches. ✓

Much better — that sounds right and it makes sense too.

Don't change When Things Happen in your writing by Mistake

This is in the <u>past</u>.　Another <u>past</u> verb.

> When our group <u>arrived</u>, the hosts <u>offered</u> everyone hot drinks — then they <u>bring</u> us homemade snacks.

This one's <u>wrong</u> — it's in the <u>present</u> when it should be <u>past</u> (i.e. 'they <u>brought</u> us homemade snacks').

Sentences don't have to be complicated — but they have to be right...

These three rules are very important. It's good to write <u>longer</u>, more <u>complicated</u> sentences, but they still have to be <u>correct</u>. When you've finished writing an answer, <u>check</u> that all your sentences make sense.

Sentences

If you really want to wow the examiner, you'll need to use different <u>types</u> of <u>sentences</u>.

Vary the Style of your sentences

Using <u>different sentence types</u> will make your writing more <u>interesting</u>. For example:

<u>Simple</u> sentences are good for <u>emphasising</u> important points. ⟹ | My cat likes pizza. |

Try adding another part in the <u>middle</u> of the sentence. ⟹ | My cat, <u>who has a wonky tail</u>, likes pizza. |

Or add <u>another part</u> to the sentence and join it
to the first part using a word like <u>and</u> or <u>but</u>. ⟹ | My cat likes pizza, <u>but he won't eat curry</u>. |

Start your sentences in Different Ways

Your writing will be pretty <u>boring</u> if all your sentences start with the same words. For example:

> <u>You can</u> play the guitar on your own or in a group. <u>You can</u> sing along with your guitar.
> <u>You can</u> make up new pieces yourself. <u>You can</u> perform on stage. ✗

It's much <u>more interesting</u> if you <u>vary</u> the way you start sentences:

> You can play the guitar on your own or in a group. You might want to try singing along with your guitar.
> Making up new pieces yourself is also possible. If you wish, you can even perform on stage. ✓

Write your sentences in a Logical Order

If you write your sentences in the wrong order, your work will be hard to understand. For example:

> When the victim left the shop, his bike had vanished. The victim went into a shop to buy a drink.

What's happening <u>isn't clear</u>, because the sentences are in the wrong order.

Try to mix up the style of your sentences...

It can also be very effective to include the occasional <u>rhetorical question</u> (p.42) in your answers to writing questions — it can help the reader feel more <u>involved</u> and keep them interested in what they're reading.

Writing Varied Sentences

When you're <u>describing</u> something you need to paint a <u>picture</u> in your reader's head — here's how.

Describe things by Comparing them to Other Things

Comparing your subject to something else helps readers to imagine it.
There are <u>three</u> ways of comparing:

1) Using less than, more than, the least, the most...

| It was beautiful. | ⟹ | It was the <u>most beautiful</u> landscape I had ever seen. |

2) You can also say something is <u>more than</u> or <u>the most</u> by adding '<u>er</u>' or '<u>est</u>' to the end, e.g. small<u>er</u>, kind<u>est</u>. But do this instead of using 'more than' or 'most'.

| Seagulls are <u>more braver than</u> other birds. ✗ | | Seagulls are <u>braver than</u> other birds. ✓ |

3) Using <u>similes</u> (to say that one thing is <u>like</u> another). You can use the words 'like' or 'as':

| The room was hot <u>like</u> the desert. | | You'll feel <u>as</u> calm <u>as</u> a gentle ocean breeze after your spa trip. |

Metaphors can create Strong Images

1) A <u>metaphor</u> describes one thing as if it <u>is</u> something else.
2) Metaphors can have a <u>very powerful effect</u>.

| The winner cried so hard that rivers flowed down his cheeks. |

There weren't really rivers flowing down the winner's cheeks, but the language creates a <u>strong visual image</u>.

It's worth practising these techniques...

We don't tend to use similes and metaphors much when we're <u>talking</u>. This means you've got to <u>practise</u> using them in your <u>writing</u> when you're revising for Section B or Unit 2 of your exams.

Writing Varied Sentences

Using lots of <u>different</u> words makes your writing more <u>interesting</u>, which is what the examiner wants...

Use **Different Words** for the **Same Thing**

Don't use the same word all the time — especially vague ones like "<u>nice</u>" or "<u>weird</u>".

I went to a <u>nice</u> Indian restaurant last night. The waiters were <u>nice</u> to us. I had a <u>nice</u> curry.

← This isn't going to score you many points because it's so <u>boring</u>.

This is loads better. Using lots of different adjectives paints a more <u>interesting picture</u>. →

I went to a <u>fantastic</u> Indian restaurant last night. The waiters were <u>friendly</u> to us. I had a <u>delicious</u> curry.

It's the same with <u>verbs</u> (doing or being words)...

These new housing developments will <u>spoil</u> our village. They will <u>spoil</u> our community spirit and <u>spoil</u> the landscape that surrounds us.

 →

These new housing developments will <u>ruin</u> our village. They will <u>destroy</u> our community spirit and <u>decimate</u> the landscape that surrounds us.

Fancy Words impress the examiner

Using <u>different</u> words is good, but if you're after top marks, try using different <u>and</u> clever words.

United played <u>badly</u> on Saturday. → United played <u>dreadfully</u> on Saturday.

The referee made some <u>very stupid</u> decisions. → The referee made some <u>incredibly moronic</u> decisions.

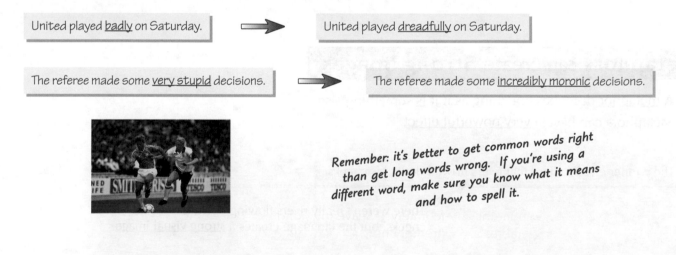

Remember: it's better to get common words right than get long words wrong. If you're using a different word, make sure you know what it means and how to spell it.

Using the same words all the time is boring...

You shouldn't use long, fancy words <u>all</u> the time — that'd sound pretty daft. But you'll get some extra <u>marks</u> if you throw them in every <u>now and then</u>. So, invest in a dictionary and learn some interesting new words.

Warm-Up Questions

Grammar's pretty tricky, so here are some lovely warm-up questions to make sure you've taken everything in. Have a really good go at them, then check your answers on p.85.

Warm-Up Questions

1) Choose the correct spelling:
   a) How you spell will <u>affect</u> / <u>effect</u> your grade.
   b) I left my bicycle over <u>their</u> / <u>there</u>.
   c) I wish I knew <u>wear</u> / <u>where</u> I was going.

2) Pick out the noun, the verb, the adjective and the adverb in each of the following sentences (sometimes there is more than one noun, verb, adjective or adverb):
   a) The enormous horses easily pulled the heavy carriages.
   b) Sonia desperately wanted to know the whole truth.
   c) The naughty little boys waited nervously outside the headteacher's office.

3) Add adverbs and adjectives to the following sentences to make them more interesting.
   a) The police car came to a stop near the wharf. The sirens continued to sound.
   b) Scruffy pulled at the lead, keen to get to the river.
   c) The room was silent. Jen looked around. There were shards of glass on the floor.

4) What's wrong with this sentence — "The children only eats sausages"?

5) Complete the following sentences by putting the verb into the correct tense:
   a) When I got home, I (turn) _____ the television on.
   b) Today, I (be) _____ happy.

6) Rewrite 5a) and 5b) so they're talking about the future.

7) Put these sentences into the correct order, from the first thing that happened to the last.
   I left completely satisfied. The crème brulée was the perfect end to a delicious meal.
   We began with a dish of lobster. The next course, beef, was well roasted and tender.

8) What three letters could you add to the word "cold" to make it mean "most cold"?

9) Which is correct?
   Katy's essay is much more better than Claire's. / Katy's essay is much better than Claire's.

10) What's the difference between a simile and a metaphor? Write an example of each.

11) Are these sentences similes or metaphors?
   a) He was as charming as a sewer rat.
   b) The clouds were a soft, white pillow.
   c) He was a mighty oak and I was just a puny pansy.
   d) The water foamed and boiled like an erupting volcano.

12) Write down three words that mean "bad".

13) Which of the following sentences uses more complex, fancy words?
   a) I go rollerblading now and then. / I go rollerblading occasionally.
   b) Evacuate the building immediately! / Leave the building now!
   c) Fruit and vegetables are extremely nutritious. / Fruit and vegetables are very healthy.

Revision Summary

There's <u>quite a lot of stuff</u> to take in here. Try these questions, check for any you got wrong and then <u>have another go</u> at them. It'll take a little while — but soon you'll slide through it all like a knife through butter...

Make Your Writing Clear to Read (p50) ☑
1) Why is it important to check through your writing?

Standard English (p51) ☑
2) Write a short paragraph to explain what Standard English is.
3) True or false: you should use dialect words, slang and text speak to write in Standard English?
4) Jot down one example of Standard English and one of non-standard English.

Punctuation (p52) ☑
5) Give one reason why you might use an exclamation mark.

Apostrophes (p53) ☑
6) Cut out letters and replace them with apostrophes. The first one is done for you.
   a) I will not = I won't   b) can not   c) I had   d) it is   e) they are
7) True or false: you should use apostrophes for plurals?

Speech Marks (p54) ☑
8) Put the speech marks in the right place in this sentence: I really need a holiday, said Martin.

Negatives (p55) ☑
9) "It's never a good idea to use no double negatives in your writing." Correct this sentence.

Spelling (p57) ☑
10) Which of these statements is correct?
    a) We where going to a fancy party.   b) I decided to wear my birthday suit.
    c) I don't know were that idea came from.

Nouns, Verbs, Adverbs and Adjectives (p58) ☑
11) Name the four kinds of noun and give two examples of each.
12) Explain the difference between adjectives and adverbs.

Using Verbs in Sentences (p59) ☑
13) Why is it important to think about verb tenses when you are writing?

Sentences (p60) ☑
14) When you are writing, why would you use sentences of different lengths?

Writing Varied Sentences (p61-62) ☑
15) When you're writing, why is it good to make comparisons between things?
16) What are two ways of using similes?
17) True or false: using different and fancy words will impress the examiner?

Practice Exam — Foundation

Once you've been through all the questions in this book, you should feel pretty confident about your English exams. Next up are some <u>practice papers</u> to really get you set for the real thing. The practice paper below is for the <u>Foundation</u> exam — you'll find a <u>Higher</u> practice paper on pages 72-77.

- Before you start, read through <u>all the instructions</u> and advice on the front of the paper.
- You'll need some paper to write your answers on.
- When you've finished, have a look at the answer section on pages 86-88 for some sample good points and answers to these questions.

CGP Practice Exam Paper
GCSE English / English Language

General Certificate of Secondary Education

GCSE
English /
English Language

Foundation Tier   **F**

Time allowed: 2 hours 15 minutes

Surname
Other names
Candidate signature

Centre name					
Centre number					
Candidate number					

Instructions to candidates
- Write your answers in **black** ink or ball-point pen.
- Write your name and other details in the boxes above.
- Answer **all** the questions in **Section A** and **Section B**.
- Cross out any rough work that you do not want to be marked.
- You need to refer to the insert booklet on pages 68-71 for this exam.
- You should **not** use a dictionary.

Information for candidates
- The marks available are given in brackets at the end of each question.
- There are 80 marks available for this exam paper.
- You must use good English and clear presentation in your answers.
- Section A will test your reading skills and Section B will test your writing skills. There are 40 marks available for each section.
- You should spend about **one hour fifteen minutes** on Section A and **one hour** on Section B.

Section A: Reading

You should answer all questions in this section.

You should spend about one hour fifteen minutes on this section.

Read **Item 1**, the newspaper article called *Record Dragons' Den investment for Harry Potter-style magic wand* and answer the questions below.

1a List 4 things the article tells you about the Kymera wand.

(4 marks)

1b What do you learn from the article about how Duncan Bannatyne is involved in the project?

(4 marks)

Read **Item 2**, the article from *Hello* magazine about Jamie Oliver, and answer the question below.

2 What reasons can you find in the article for saying that Jamie Oliver is a successful chef and helps people and animals?

(8 marks)

Read **Item 3**, an extract called 'Local Customs' from a government guide called *Travel Safe*, and answer the question below.

3 How does the writer use language to inform and advise travellers about local customs?

(12 marks)

Now look again at all three items. They have each been presented in an interesting way.

4 Choose **two** of these items. Compare them using these headings:

- The layout of the text

- The use of pictures

(12 marks)

Section B: Writing

You should answer **both** questions in this section.

You should spend about one hour on this section. You should spend about twenty-five minutes on question 5 and about thirty-five minutes on question 6.

---

5   Write a letter to a friend describing your favourite celebrity
    and explaining why you like this person.

(16 marks)

6   You have been asked to make a speech to your local town council persuading
    them to improve road safety near your school. Your speech should include:

    •   what makes the road unsafe now

    •   how you think road safety could be improved

    •   why improving road safety near your school is important

(24 marks)

CGP Practice Exam Paper
GCSE English / English Language

General Certificate of Secondary Education

F

GCSE
English / English Language

Foundation Tier

Insert

The three items that follow are:

- **ITEM 1:** *Record Dragons' Den investment for Harry Potter-style magic wand,* an article from The Daily Telegraph

- **ITEM 2:** an article from *Hello* magazine about Jamie Oliver

- **ITEM 3:** an extract called 'Local Customs' from a government guide called *Travel Safe*

ITEM 1

Record Dragons' Den investment for Harry Potter-style magic wand

A Harry Potter-style wand that can change television channels with the flick of a wrist has attracted a record investment from Dragons' Den, the BBC2 show for entrepreneurs.

Laura Roberts
Wednesday, 25 August 2010
The Telegraph

Chris Barnardo with the Kymera Wand

Duncan Bannatyne invested £200,000 in the wand which can be customised to control a variety of household electronic appliances such as laptops, light switches, televisions, hi-fis, DVD players and even remote-controlled curtains.

The Kymera wand, a buttonless remote control, was invented by Chris Barnardo and Richard Blakesley who set up The Wand Company. The entrepreneurs* entered the Dragons' Den in a bid to get further investment for the product which can be tuned into 13 different devices and activated using different gestures.

Mr Barnardo and Mr Blakesley were offered a combined total of £900,000 by the Dragons for the 14-inch wand and accepted investment from Mr Bannatyne in return for 20 per cent of the business.

Mr Barnardo, 47, of Bishop's Stortford, Herts., said: "We planned our pitch very carefully and looked at the presentations of hundreds of previous entrants.

"We expected that we would be questioned strongly so we prepared our answers. When they all put their money in it was a real thrill.

"The whole thing was knee wobblingly scary and I'm not ashamed to admit that I was very nervous. It was terrifying when £900,000 was on the table.

"We are looking forward very much to working with Duncan because of his vast business experience."

The £49.95 Kymera Wand uses movement control technology similar to the Nintendo Wii, and can "learn" up to 13 infra-red codes from existing remotes and assign each command a gesture.

Owners will be able to turn up the volume by rotating the wand or change channel with a flick of the wrist.

Different moves can also be assigned to different gadgets, so the same wand can control a variety of devices.

The wand runs on two AAA batteries and enters a low-power "sleep mode" after 60 seconds of inactivity.

It uses a three-axis accelerometer* to detect movement, similar to technology in mobile phones where a picture turns to remain upright when the phone is rotated.

A tiny piece of silicon the size of a grain of sugar detects which way up the wand is and interprets its movements.

The inventors have already sold over 20,000 Kymera Wands since the launch in September last year and it is now on sale in 41 countries.

They expect to turnover £2 million in the next year with the help of Mr Bannatyne.

The Dragon said: "I see the magic wand rolling out very quickly over the next six months and I think it will do very, very well."

© Telegraph Media Group Limited 2010

*entrepreneur — someone who starts and runs their own business

*accelerometer — device that measures how fast something speeds up

ITEM 2

Jamie Oliver

© Nils Jorgensen/REX/Shutterstock

Born on May 27, 1975, Jamie grew up above his parents' Essex pub *The Cricketers*, where he helped in the kitchens as a tot, and experimented with his mum's Aga cooker when she wasn't looking. It was an early training which was to prove useful when he left school at 16 to attend Westminster Catering College.

Jobs at several prestigious* restaurants in England and the rest of Europe followed. And by the time Pat Llewelyn, producer of the *Two Fat Ladies* TV cookery show contacted him after spotting him in a documentary about the *Riverside Café*, he had already risen to the level of sous-chef at the prestigious London eatery.

When the tousle-haired maestro stormed onto the TV cooking scene with his programme *The Naked Chef* critics were initially bemused by the 21-year-old's accent and presenting style. But they were soon forced to accept that audiences loved his simple, fun food, and good natured wide-boy persona.

The Essex-boy-done-great eventually caught the eye of British premier Tony Blair, who asked him to whip up an appropriately themed dinner for a meeting with the PM's Italian counterpart. The result was such a success the Labour leader offered Jamie the job of "food tsar" for Britain's hospitals, a role he declined.

He's a millionaire, was voted People magazine's sexiest chef, and is happily married to his childhood sweetheart. Life has been kind to celebrity cook Jamie Oliver.

Protective of his street cred image, *The Naked Chef* star has refused to endorse* international food and beverage giants whose product or marketing strategy do not meet with his approval. Both Nestle and Coca-Cola who asked him to pose naked for an ad campaign have been rebuffed.

Wanting to put his high-profile status to good use, the big-hearted chef opened a charity restaurant in London called Fifteen. As part of a TV show, called *Jamie's Kitchen*, he trained fifteen disadvantaged youngsters to work in the catering field. The show was a hit, and other Fifteen restaurants have been opened across the world.

Then in 2005 Jamie launched his hugely successful *Jamie's School Dinners* series, in which he campaigned to get healthier food on the menu in school canteens. Thanks to his efforts the government pledged to spend £280m on school dinners over the course of the next three years and Jamie was voted the year's most inspiring political figure at a high-profile awards ceremony.

Having overturned the school dinners industry the health conscious chef turned his attentions to highlighting the plight of battery-farmed chickens in the poultry industry. He launched *Jamie's Fowl Dinners*, and, following his exposé, supermarkets reported massive increases in the sales of organic and free-range chickens.

His personal life is just as successful. Jamie married ex-model Juliette "Jules" Norton whom he met while they were both still students at Newport Free Grammar school in a church just 200 metres from his parents' home. Key to the ceremony was a performance by an Elvis impersonator who sang *I Can't Help Falling In Love*. Jamie and Jules enjoy home life with their children.

*prestigious — well-known
*endorse — advertise

ITEM 3

LOCAL CUSTOMS

Meeting local people and getting to grips with a country's customs and culture is one of the delights of travel. Most of us know not to show the soles of our feet when in Thailand, but many a traveller has been left standing at the bar due to the mysterious art of tipping in American bars. On the other hand, you'll get a lot of cups of tea bought for you by strangers in the Middle East, and may never work out how to buy any back in return. Of course some types of behaviour will be universally badly received — dressing inappropriately, loudly expressing political views and criticising your host country will never go down well. Good manners are always appreciated.

While local customs vary from country to country, the solution to any unwittingly delivered faux-pas* is a smile and a polite apology. Most people you'll meet will know you're not versed in local custom and be pleased to gently put you right.

5 unusual customs

• In Russia and Central Asia vodka plays a part in most social rituals — expect many toasts and a headache in the morning.

• In Madagascar it is considered *fady* (taboo) to point with an outstretched finger.

• The popular Afghan sport of Buzkashi involves men on horseback battling for the carcass of a headless goat.

• Land diving, an early form of bungee jumping, was invented on Vanuatu in the South Pacific where men hurl themselves off a platform with vines tied around their ankles — all in the name of ensuring a good yam harvest.

• If you didn't know it already, you'll soon find out that ribbing Poms, normally about sport, is a national pastime for Australians and Kiwis!

Sometimes you'll encounter surprising behaviour from local people directed at you. In China, foreigners are greeted with cries of 'Longwai!'; in East Africa the cry is 'Mzungu' and in Thailand 'Farang'. The shouts are various terms to describe outsiders, foreigners and Europeans, and may follow you around on your visit to the country. While these shouts are normally accompanied by big smiles it can be a challenge to remain good humoured. The best strategy is to treat such comments as a mixture of a joke, and a gesture of recognition and curiosity — no harm is meant.

The best way to get in tune with the local customs is to immerse yourself* and expect your first few days to be something of a culture shock. Before you go you can get a handle on what to expect by reading guidebooks, chatting to other travellers and checking out FCO Travel Advice (www.gov.uk/foreign-travel-advice). While it pays to be prepared, remember that discovering the richness of local cultures is one of the great joys of travel.

*faux-pas — social mistake
*immerse yourself — get fully involved

72

Practice Exam — Higher

Here's another <u>practice exam</u> to test how well-prepared you are for the real thing. This time, it's for the <u>Higher</u> exam — you'll find the <u>Foundation</u> practice paper on pages 65-71.

- Before you start, read through <u>all the instructions</u> and advice on the front of the paper.
- You'll need some paper to write your answers on.
- When you've finished, have a look at the answers on pages 88-90 — they'll give you some ideas of the kind of things you should have included in your answers.

CGP Practice Exam Paper
GCSE English / English Language

General Certificate of Secondary Education

GCSE
English /
English Language

Higher Tier   **H**

Time allowed: 2 hours 15 minutes

Surname	
Other names	
Candidate signature	

Centre name				
Centre number				
Candidate number				

Instructions to candidates
- Write your answers in **black** ink or ball-point pen.
- Write your name and other details in the boxes above.
- Answer **all** the questions in **Section A** and **Section B**.
- Cross out any rough work that you do not want to be marked.
- You need to refer to the insert booklet on pages 74-77 for this exam.
- You should **not** use a dictionary.

Information for candidates
- The marks available are given in brackets at the end of each question.
- There are 80 marks available for this exam paper.
- You must use good English and clear presentation in your answers.
- Section A will test your reading skills and Section B will test your writing skills. There are 40 marks available for each section.
- You should spend about **one hour fifteen minutes** on Section A and **one hour** on Section B.

Section A: Reading

You should answer all questions in this section.

You should spend about one hour fifteen minutes on this section.

Read **Item 1**, the article *Piece of Isaac Newton's apple tree to experience zero gravity in space*.

1   What do you learn from the article about what Piers Sellers is doing and why he wants to do it?

(8 marks)

Now read **Item 2**, the online article *Be Inspired*, which is about the city of Oxford.

2   How do the pictures and layout help to make the text effective?

(8 marks)

Now read **Item 3**, an extract from *The Diving Bell and the Butterfly*, which is a non-fiction book.

3   What are some of the narrator's thoughts and feelings?

(8 marks)

Now you need to refer to **Item 3**, the extract from *The Diving Bell and the Butterfly* and **either** Item 1 **or** Item 2. You are going to compare the texts, one of which you have chosen.

4   Compare the ways in which the writers use language to achieve their purpose in the two texts.

(16 marks)

Section B: Writing

You should answer **both** questions in this section.

You should spend about one hour on this section. You should spend about twenty-five minutes on question 5 and about thirty-five minutes on question 6.

---

5   There is a member of your family whom you would particularly like a friend to meet. Write a letter to your friend explaining which family member you would like him or her to meet and why.

(16 marks)

6   'The media should not bother us with the private lives of celebrities, their families and their partners.' Write an article for a newspaper or magazine which argues for or against this idea.

(24 marks)

CGP Practice Exam Paper
GCSE English / English Language

General Certificate of Secondary Education

H

GCSE
English / English Language

Higher Tier

Insert

The three items that follow are:

- **ITEM 1:** an article, *Piece of Isaac Newton's apple tree to experience zero gravity in space*

- **ITEM 2:** an online article, *Be Inspired*, about the city of Oxford.

- **ITEM 3:** an extract from *The Diving Bell and the Butterfly* by Jean-Dominique Bauby

ITEM 1

Piece of Isaac Newton's apple tree to experience zero gravity in space

Jacqui Goddard, Miami
May 10 2010

When Sir Isaac Newton saw an apple fall from a tree, its downward motion led him to one of the greatest scientific discoveries - the theory of gravitation. Three centuries later, a British astronaut is set to take a piece of the same tree on a gravity-defying mission in the opposite direction.

Photograph: ©iStock.com/graphicola

Piers Sellers, who will be the last Briton to fly on a space shuttle when Atlantis blasts off on its final mission later this week, has packed a four-inch sliver of wood from the tree that inspired the 17th-century physicist in the spaceship's hold.

The historic memento has been entrusted to Mr Sellers by the Royal Society, of which Sir Isaac was once president, as part of its 350th anniversary celebrations. It will accompany him on his 4.9 million-mile voyage to and from the International Space Station.

"While it's up there, it will be experiencing no gravity, so if it had an apple on it the apple wouldn't fall. I'm pretty sure that Sir Isaac would have loved to see this, assuming he wasn't spacesick, as it would have proved his first law of motion to be correct," said Mr Sellers, 55.

Fulfilling Sir Isaac's observation that what goes up must come down, Mr Sellers will return the artifact to the Royal Society following his mission, to be placed on permanent display.

"I'll take it up into orbit and let it float around a bit, which will confuse Isaac, and bring it back and give it to the society," he said.

"This is from the apple tree, the one he was looking at when the apple fell down and he got the idea...That's something, isn't it?" Keith Moore, head librarian at the Royal Society, confirmed that the section comes from the apple tree that still stands in Sir Isaac's one-time home, Woolsthorpe Manor, in Lincolnshire.

"It's a fun thing. Piers approached us to take something up and we were faced with the question 'What might that be, what would be appropriate?' Of course the apple tree immediately hooked into our minds because of gravity. Once you are up in space you can begin to demonstrate Newton's laws of motion," he said.

"The idea is that this will inspire people. You can begin to talk to schoolchildren about science and its theories, you want to inspire that next generation of scientists, physicists, mathematicians - and even astronauts." Mr Sellers was born in Crowborough, East Sussex, educated at Cranbrook School in Kent and attended university in Edinburgh and Leeds. He was selected for Nasa's elite astronaut corps in 1996 and has flown two previous shuttle missions, logging just over 559 hours in space.

His wife Mandy, originally from Hebden Bridge in Yorkshire, and children Imogen, 24, and Tom, 22, will be watching as Atlantis lifts off from Cape Canaveral in Florida this Friday on its swansong mission. Its sister-ships, Discovery and Endeavour, are each due to make one more flight later this year before the fleet goes into retirement. Under President Barack Obama's new vision for Nasa, plans for a successor spacecraft have been cancelled.

"These are the three surviving shuttles out of five, beautiful, very complicated machines - about three million parts in each of them... They'll be in museums and be revered. People will go there and say 'Wow, there's the first space plane, look at that,'" said Mr Sellers.

"But I'm not one of those who feels sad about it. I think we should wind up the shuttle programme pretty soon, while we're ahead. They've done tremendous work for the US space programme and international partners, and they've done good service. It's time to move in to the next thing."

© The Times
May 10th 2010 / nisyndication.com

ITEM 2

Be In*spired*

© iStock.com/Snowshill

Oxford — just an hour on the train from the heart of London, a visit to this hive of history, culture and education is sure to leave you satisfied. Whether you're after a lazy picnic in Port Meadow, a whistle-stop tour of the university, or simply the chance to grab a coffee and indulge in a bit of retail therapy — Oxford is the place to be. The city's pretty colleges and quadrangles are clustered together, so once you've arrived you'll be free to wander the quaint, cobbled lanes and seek out some of the city's best kept secrets. If you haven't got time to explore the city at a leisurely pace, why not hire a bicycle or a punt for a cheap chance to see Oxford from a different perspective?

> Accommodation

> Getting here

> Arts and Theatre

> Shopping

> Museums

> Eating out

> The University

> Exploring Oxfordshire

The ancient university

Without doubt, the jewel in the crown of this historic city is its university — the oldest in the English-speaking world. It's famous for schooling some of the world's most celebrated minds and has produced leaders in fields as diverse as politics, science and literature. Hundreds of years of tradition are waiting to welcome you, and the university still leads the way in many of its departments — research carried out here is second to none and is at the forefront of academic advancement. Around the start and end of the academic year, you'll be able to see students around the town in traditional academic dress, which provides great photo opportunities. Also, if you can drag yourself from the comfort of one of Oxford's superb hotels for an early start, you shouldn't miss the opportunity to watch the college and university rowing teams training on the water before their lectures begin.

© iStock.com/stocknshares

Founded in 1379, New College is one of the stunning Oxford colleges open to the public. Click on the video link above for a virtual tour.

© iStock.com/Edward Shaw

Christ Church Cathedral — one of many places in Oxford where open space, relaxation and history go hand in hand.

A modern metropolis

Oxford seamlessly merges the traditional with the modern. Academic gowns that have been traditional for centuries are worn by teenage students talking on their mobiles, and centuries-old pubs can be found nestled between high-street giants and international chains. As a result, Oxford offers unrivalled variety to shoppers and diners — there are scores of independent shops, cafés and restaurants as well as the big names you'd expect to find on any high street. Whatever you're looking for, chances are you'll be able to find it here.

Open spaces in the city

The Botanic Garden, tucked away on the south side of Magdalen Bridge, offers an oasis of tranquillity if the buzz of the high street is not your thing. It boasts a startling selection of 7,000 different species of plants. The garden, along with the nearby Harcourt arboretum, is well worth a look for any green-fingered visitors or for those who simply appreciate fresh air and open space. Alternatively, the University Parks, Christ Church Meadow and Port Meadow all provide plenty of room to relax or take the kids to let off some steam.

The 19th-century poet Matthew Arnold described Oxford as the city of 'dreaming spires', so what better way to round off your visit than by looking down over the city from one of its tallest towers? From the top of the University Church of St Mary the Virgin you are treated to a 360-degree panorama, which allows you to see down into the private grounds of the surrounding colleges and gives stunning views of famous landmarks, such as the Radcliffe Camera, the Bridge of Sighs and the Examination Schools.

History. Culture. Education. Oxford has it all!

ITEM 3

In this extract the author describes spending Father's Day at the beach with his children after he has suffered a stroke that has left him almost entirely paralysed.

Hunched in my wheelchair, I surreptitiously watch my children as their mother pushes me down the hospital corridor. While I have become something of a zombie father, Théophile and Céleste are very much flesh and blood, energetic and noisy. I will never tire of seeing them walk alongside me, just walking, their confident expressions masking the unease weighing on their small shoulders. As he walks, Théophile dabs with a Kleenex at the thread of saliva escaping my closed lips. His movements are tentative, at once tender and fearful, as if he were dealing with an unpredictable animal. As soon as we slow down, Céleste cradles my head in her bare arms, covers my forehead with noisy kisses and says over and over, 'You're my dad, you're my dad,' as if in incantation.

Today is Father's Day. Until my stroke we had felt no need to fit this made-up holiday into our emotional calendar. But this time we spent the whole of this symbolic day together, affirming that even a rough sketch, a shadow, a tiny fragment of a dad is still a dad. I am torn between joy at seeing them living, moving, laughing or crying for a few hours, and fear that the sight of all these sufferings – beginning with mine – is not the ideal entertainment for a boy of ten and his eight-year-old sister. However, we have made the wise collective decision not to sugarcoat anything.

We install ourselves at the Beach Club – my name for a patch of sand-dune open to sun and wind, where the hospital has obligingly set out tables, chairs and umbrellas, and even planted a few buttercups which grow in the sand amid the weeds. In this neutral zone on the beach, a transition between hospital and everyday life, one could easily imagine some good fairy turning every wheelchair into a chariot. 'Want to play hangman?' asks Théophile, and I ache to tell him that I have enough on my plate playing quadriplegic. But my communication system disqualifies repartee: the keenest rapier grows dull and falls flat when it takes several minutes to thrust it home. By the time you strike, even you no longer understand what had seemed so witty before you started to dictate it, letter by letter. So the rule is to avoid impulsive sallies. It deprives conversation of its sparkle, all those gems you bat back and forth like a ball – and I count this forced lack of humour one of the great drawbacks of my condition.

But we can certainly play hangman, the national pre-teen sport. I guess a letter, then another, then stumble on the third. My heart is not in the game. Grief surges over me. His face not two feet from mine, my son Théophile sits patiently waiting – and I, his father, have lost the simple right to ruffle his bristly hair, clasp his downy neck, hug his small, lithe, warm body tight against me. There are no words to express it. My condition is monstrous, iniquitous, revolting, horrible. Suddenly, I can take no more. Tears well and my throat emits a hoarse rattle that startles Théophile. Don't be scared, little man, I love you. Still engrossed in the game, he moves in for the kill. Two more letters: he has won, and I have lost. On a corner of the page he completes his drawing of the gallows, the rope and the condemned man.

Some answers are broken up into bullet points (•) to give you an idea of the type of points you could make in your answer. These are only intended to give you an idea of what you should be writing — there are many different possible answers.

Page 15 — Warm-Up Questions

1) It's best to read the question before you read the text, so you know exactly what information to look for.

2) You can make it obvious by rephrasing the words of the question in your first sentence.

3)
*   The website's colour scheme is the first thing to catch the reader's eye, and gets them in the right frame of mind for the website's purpose: looking for love. The varying tones of pink and the contrasting blue are associated with women and men. Pink is a warm colour that is traditionally associated with romance, so it supports the text's purpose. The colour pink on the left of the page draws attention to the 'Editor's pick' section, where users' personal advertisements are positioned. The pink and blue bars at the top and bottom of the page match the colours in the photographs to the right, creating a sense of order in the colour scheme.

4)
*   The Lonely Hearts Club website suggests that the organisation wants to achieve three main things. The first aim is to 'matchmake' the website's users. This is made clear in the first sentence of the 'About Us' section, in the line, "helping people across the world find their soulmate." This makes the company sound well-established and like they have helped a lot of people, which makes the reader trust them, and supports the purpose of the text — to persuade people to use their service.

*   The Lonely Hearts Club's second aim is to offer a variety of ways for single people to communicate. The website lists various tools to use to talk to other people looking for love: adverts, instant messaging and the company's own software, 'Matchmaker'. If the website's users can easily chat to one another, they are more likely to find people they match well with, giving the Lonely Hearts Club a higher success rate and persuading more people to use them.

*   Lonely Hearts Club's third aim is to carefully match couples who are well suited to one another. The website text includes technical-sounding words, such as "expertly tailored" and "accurately", to make it seem as if there is a trustworthy and scientific basis to their methods of matchmaking. This is supported by the real-life examples of the weddings that the writer claims to be invited to each week. By using specialised language, the writer makes Lonely Hearts Club sound reliable and trusted by satisfied customers.

5)
*   The website has four main graphics: a logo, a playing card and two polaroid photographs. They combine with the colour scheme and the layout to create a welcoming and attractive page that informs the reader about what the company does.

*   The logo is pink, which is traditionally associated with romance and love. The cartoon-like hearts and the chunky text balance out the formality of the font used for the word 'Club', and together they create the effect of a professional but friendly dating company, which persuades people to use the service.

*   The playing card features a single heart which echoes the idea of 'lonely hearts'. Playing cards are used by magicians — so it could also make the reader think that something 'magical' might happen to them if they use the site. Again, this supports the website's purpose, to persuade people to use the service.

*   Finally, the polaroid photographs act as proof of the website's success. They have been designed to look like 'real' photographs of 'real' people that have used the website's service, and prove that the text is not just making empty claims. This effect is made stronger by the fact that the photographs are labelled with the first names of the couples, showing that they are real people. The contrast in age of the people in the two photographs ensures that the website has a broad appeal. James and Melanie are looking directly at the reader, which draws them in, and Edith and Harris are looking at one another, which shows the affection between them. Both couples are smiling, which makes the reader feel that they can be happy if they use this site. This gives the message that the site can help you find true love, so visitors are more likely to use the company.

6)
*   The second website is less formal than Lonely Hearts Club's, due to its use of language, voice and sentence structure. The website for Lonely Hearts Club uses technical language like "instant messaging" to explain how users can "meet" online (written in inverted commas as if it is an unusual idea), whereas the second website assumes its readers understand and use less technical language. For instance, it does not directly refer to software when it claims it will "search heaven and earth," which suggests that it hopes to appeal to a younger, more computer-literate audience.

*   Both websites are written in the first-person, which makes them sound familiar and friendly. Lonely Hearts Club's first-person voice is warm but serious, and full, complex sentences make the voice sound more professional than chatty. However, the second website uses a less formal voice and mimics spoken language ("Bliss!") to make the reader feel as if they are being addressed personally by the "Stupid Cupid".

Page 16 — Foundation Exam Questions

1) Any four from:
- Hutches/cages should be brought to a quiet room indoors or put into a garage or shed.
- Small pets should be given extra bedding.
- Hutches that can't be brought inside should be turned to face a wall or fence.
- Aviaries or hutches should be covered with thick blankets or duvets to block out the sight and muffle the sound of fireworks.
- Dogs and cats should be kept inside.
- Dogs should be walked earlier in the day before the fireworks begin.
- Windows and doors should be closed and catflaps blocked to stop pets getting out and to keep noise down.
- TVs and radios should be switched on if pets are used to them to help block out the noise of the fireworks.
- Dogs should be given ID tags. Pet owners should consider microchips in case their pets run away.
- Owners should prepare dens for their pets so they have somewhere safe and comfortable to hide.

2) Answers should include at least four of the following points:
- Fireworks cause many animals to suffer.
- Some end up needing medication due to the stress caused by fireworks.
- Many animals run away from home during bonfire night.
- Animals have "acute hearing", so the loud noises caused by fireworks can cause them pain.
- Small pets are "easily frightened" by noises like fireworks.
- Small pets need "special care" when fireworks are let off.

3)

Amazing experiences
- The article shows that Mike Perham had many amazing experiences. As the headline points out he became the "youngest person to sail round the world solo". This means that no one else had done it which is an amazing experience in itself.
- The article quotes him as saying at the end of his trip: "I am absolutely ecstatic. It feels amazing." This makes it seem that Mike Perham himself feels that the trip has been an amazing experience.
- He also describes experiences he will "never forget" such as "seeing hundreds of dolphins at once", which is something most people never get to see.
- He describes some of the beautiful things he saw, such as "incredible sunsets", which make the experience sound amazing and worthwhile.

- The article ends with a quote from his father saying that Mike "is a very special son" and has done "incredibly well". This suggests that his father thinks that his son has done an amazing thing.

Difficult times
- Early in the article, the writer mentions some "euphemistic "Oh crikey!" moments". This suggests that there were many points when things went wrong.
- Even when things went right, it seems that the journey itself was a difficult one. Mike Perham says in the article that the "ongoing low" was always being on his own.
- The writer uses the rule of three when describing what Mike Perham had to face on his voyage: "50ft waves, gale-force winds and a couple of hair-raising "knockdowns"". This makes the problems he faced seem difficult and relentless.
- The article also includes a description of "another drama" where Mike Perham had to make "30-second dives for 40 minutes in the Pacific". This shows how specific events were difficult and dangerous for him.
- The article includes examples of "horrendous" weather such as "50-knot winds" which shows that Mike Perham had to face extreme challenges.

4) See Worked Exam Answer on page 20.

5)
- Item 1 uses pictures to make us feel sympathetic towards the animals. The cat on the front cover of the website article is buried in its bedding, which makes it look as if it might be worried. The cat on the third page of the leaflet is staring out as if it is panicking.
- The picture of the cat on the third page also illustrates the point the leaflet makes about preparing a "den" for your pet, so it shows how owners can protect their animals.
- Item 3 uses a picture of a run-down building to show that Hector and his family's living conditions are bad.
- The other photo shows some of the children in the family in their home. This shows the reader some of the people from the article and gives them an idea of the kind of conditions they live in.
- Both pictures in Item 3 show how bad conditions are and make the reader feel sympathy for Hector and his family, so the reader will be more likely to give money to the charity.
- The main title of Item 1 is "Fireworks and animals". This is informative as it sets out clearly what the main theme of the leaflet is. Putting these two things close together in one sentence grabs the reader's attention, as most people know that animals need to be kept away from fireworks.
- The main title of Item 3 is "When Danger Starts at Home". This is an attention-grabbing title because we normally think of "home" as being a safe place, but here it's made to seem a really dangerous place.

- The subtitles in Item 1 make it easier for readers to use the leaflet, as owners of small pets or dogs and cats are directed to the part of the leaflet that will help them.

- The subheading text under the main title in Item 3 makes it clear that the writer is asking for action on the part of the reader, as it says "Please help me". The word "please" makes the appeal sound more urgent, and the word "me" makes a personal appeal from the writer to the reader. The subtitle also shows that the money will help improve people's lives "for good". This means the reader is persuaded to donate, because their money will help provide long-term solutions to the problem, rather than a quick fix.

Page 21 — Higher Exam Questions

1)

- From the leaflet, we learn that Plan International is a charity that tries to help children in the poorest parts of the world escape from poverty. Their focus on children is shown in the leaflet when they say that they "put children at the very heart" of their work. The phrase "at the very heart" means right at the centre, suggesting that children are the main priority for the charity. The leaflet also states that the charity tries to give children "the skills and knowledge they need to make the most of their lives". This shows one of the main ways that the charity achieves their aim of helping children — by giving them information and skills that they could use to improve their current situations.

- Plan International also helps children by allowing people to write to the child they sponsor, in order to "encourage" them. For example, Filifing, a child helped by Plan International, was "inspired" by "messages of encouragement" from her sponsor. Through this example, the leaflet suggests that these messages can help keep sponsored children motivated, so they are more likely to achieve their goals.

- The leaflet also suggests that Plan International helps to fight poverty in wider communities, not just child poverty. The text states that the charity provides communities with "clean water, nourishing food, healthcare and education". Giving people water, food and healthcare helps them survive and be healthy, and giving them education means that they will have more opportunities in life, and therefore stand a better chance of escaping from poverty. Ultimately, this also helps support the charity's main aim of helping children, as they will be surrounded by a healthier, happier and better-off community.

2)

- The headline of the article is in a larger font and in two different colours, which makes it stand out. This makes it really clear what the article is about at a glance. The words "New York" are written in quite a blocky, modern font with straight edges rather than curves, which echoes the shape of the buildings shown in the left-hand photo.

- The text box in the top left corner of the page is brightly coloured, which attracts the reader's eye and informs them that the article falls under the category of "travel". This makes its target audience clear — we know it's aimed at potential travellers/people interested in travel. The colours used in the three images, however, are darker, night-time shades, giving an adult and sophisticated impression and making the article attractive to the reader.

- The article uses subheadings like "Sleep" and "To do", which help to break the article up and make the information easier to take in. The subheadings also make it easy for readers to skip to the bit of the article that they are particularly interested in, and find out what they want to know, including how to book their own trip. In this way, the article is persuasive, as well as informative, because it encourages readers to stay at the hotel.

- Images are used to support the persuasive nature of the text, by making New York look modern and exciting. The lit buildings in the two smaller photos make New York look inviting and lively, which makes people more likely to visit. The main image, of a model looking stylish and dressed fashionably, shows that New York is a "glamorous" destination — the hotel is associated with the magazine's fashion shoot and "classic New York style".

3)

- At the beginning of the extract, the narrator is focused on the practicalities of his situation, and this is reflected in his use of phrases such as "I decided". However, he also compares the ridge he has climbed to a "flying buttress on a Gothic cathedral" and uses words like "transfixed", suggesting that the landscape fills him with awe, and that he has spiritual feelings about the mountain.

- The principal emotion in the first paragraph is loneliness. The narrator says, "I'd never felt so alone, ever." Using both "never" and "ever" here emphasises that this isn't an ordinary loneliness, it is complete isolation from all human contact. This is supported by the list of ordinary activities that he imagines people doing: "watching baseball", "eating fried chicken", "drinking beer, making love", which shows that he feels isolated not only by distance, but also by what he is doing, which is outside most people's experience or understanding. There is also a sense that he envies the lives he is imagining.

- The narrator's "troubled dreams" show that he is uneasy, and fears for his life. This sense of unease increases when he wakes up and sees "a dark line of squalls", meaning that he has to "reach the summit and make it back down before the weather turned." This suggests that the climb could become more difficult and dangerous, which creates a feeling of anxiety. He says he strapped his crampons on "hurriedly" and was climbing "Five minutes after waking up", which emphasises the fact that he feels pressured to beat the bad weather.

- This feeling of anxiety and the need for speed continues throughout the rest of the extract. The narrator says he "scurried", suggesting that he feels like a small animal, and he was "continually out of breath". These words highlight his feeling of urgency and fear as he is pursued by the "racing" storm front.

- Despite this, the climbing is "almost fun", and the narrator is clearly relishing the physical challenge. However, this changes in the final paragraph, when his main feeling is once again one of anxiety as he is unable to find a hold for his ice ax, which he describes as "a reprise of my first attempt". This shows that he fears that this attempt, like his first attempt, will fail, which suggests that he is reliving bad memories. His fear of falling also shows in his physical responses, he says "My stomach churned", which shows how terrifying he is finding it, and contrasts with his earlier feeling that it is "almost fun".

4)

- Item 1 has been written to inform and persuade. The text uses facts and statistics such as "one in five children will die before their fifth birthday", which makes it sound knowledgeable and well-informed. This causes the reader to trust the author, and makes them more likely to donate money. In contrast, Item 3 is written to inform and entertain. For this reason, it uses fewer facts than Item 1, and uses them in a very different way. For example, Item 3 starts with the words "On the afternoon of May 15", which makes it seem like a diary entry. This gives it a very personal quality, and makes the reader feel that they have access to the narrator's private thoughts and feelings, which makes it more interesting.

- Item 1 uses emotive language like "incredible hardship" and "weakened" to provoke strong feelings in the reader and make them pity the children who are suffering. Short sentences like "It is unjust" are designed to shock the reader and make them feel that something needs to be done. Again, this is a persuasive tactic, because it plays on the reader's emotions and encourages them to make a donation to change the children's lives. Item 3 uses more descriptive language, which paints a picture for the reader and allows them to visualise the scene more easily. For example, the narrator describes "the storm front racing in from the Pacific, darkening the sky",

which conveys his sense of fear and paints a picture for the reader of how dangerous his situation was. He also focuses on all the things he doesn't have — he has "no rope, no tent or bivouac gear, no hardware". This reminds the reader of how different the narrator's experience is to their own, and makes them fear for his safety, which makes them want to keep reading to find out what happened next. Like Item 1, Item 3 uses short sentences, such as "My stomach churned.", but here they have the effect of showing the narrator's fear and building suspense.

- Parts of Item 1 use the first person, e.g. "Today, over 80,000 people in the UK alone sponsor children with us" and "Throughout our history, we've put children at the very heart of our work". By using "us", "our" and "we", the text highlights the work that the charity does, and also makes it sound caring, so the reader feels as if the charity deserves their donation. In places, the text also uses second-person pronouns, e.g. "So you'll touch not just one child's life, but the lives of their families, friends and neighbours too". This persuades the reader to donate to the charity by addressing them directly, which makes them feel more involved and suggests that their personal sponsorship money will have a direct impact. Item 3, on the other hand, uses the first person to focus the text on the narrator's experiences. For example, the narrator says "I decided to spend the night there". Lots of the sentences in Item 3 start with the word "I", which emphasises that the narrator is alone, and that the story he is telling really happened to him. This makes the reader trust what he is saying and feel personally involved with him, which makes the text more gripping.

- Item 1 uses repetition of fairly simple language to persuade the reader, whereas Item 3 uses more varied, complex language. In Item 1, the word "plan" is repeated several times, e.g. "It's a plan that works — and a plan that you'll see in action". 'Plan' is the charity's name, so repeating it means that the reader will remember the charity later on. The repetition also emphasises the charity's key message, which is that it has a good plan to help children, and makes the charity sound organised, reassuring the reader that their money will be used well. This supports the main purpose of the article, which is to persuade people to sponsor children. In contrast, Item 3 uses a range of more complex vocabulary, such as "crampons" and "bivouac". This makes the writer's experiences more interesting because it shows the high level of technical knowledge and ability required to complete his climb, making it seem impressive. It also makes the writer's descriptions more engaging for the reader, because the language is varied and unusual.

Page 43 — Warm-Up Questions

1)

- Dear Michael Pea,

  I was extremely disappointed by the news that the council have decided to continue with the plans to close Dalebridge youth centre in order to fund the construction of the new shopping area in town. I believe that this decision is unwise and shortsighted. Many local young people value the youth centre, and make use of its clubs and societies on a daily basis. The self-defence class, for instance, has trebled in size since last December, and the cheerleading classes remain as popular as ever. Without this centre, young people would have no access to the organised evening activities which have proved so successful in improving school attendance and lowering anti-social behaviour in the area.

2)

- It is not often that I have anything bad to say about the golden series that is 'Definitely Ballroom'. The discerning viewer expects certain things from established prime-time shows like this, and 'Definitely Ballroom' always delivers the goods. But this week, instead of the top-notch production that I look forward to, the show was ruined by garish costumes and clumsy dancing. What's more, the pace of the show was extremely slow. It was a total let down and I am disappointed with the producers of the show, who usually work so hard to dazzle their audience.

3)

- I urge you to vote for me as class representative because I am a dependable and hardworking candidate pledging to:
  - campaign for a new drinks machine
  - negotiate more non-uniform days
  - put a stop to detentions for being late before the register is closed.

4)

- Dear Kath,

  I thought I'd send you a little postcard to let you know we're all having a brilliant time here in Blackpool. I've been on the big rollercoaster twice; it was one of the most terrifying things I've ever done, but it's so much fun! It goes so high that you can see the tower and the beach from the top. Tomorrow, we're going to ride the donkeys and go for chips on the pier.

  How are you? I hope all is well back home. I'm looking forward to catching up when I get back. I can't wait to hear all the gossip!
  Love from Rosie

5)

- Using public transport is better for the environment as it lowers the amount of fuel emissions released into the atmosphere.
- It is often cheaper to use public transport than to pay the cost of filling up the car with petrol.
- If more people use public transport the level of congestion on the roads will decrease, so people will get to their destinations faster.

6)

- Dear Mum — Just thought I should write a little note to explain why I'd really like to get a dog. I'm not just thinking of myself because you would be able to take the dog for walks as well as me. This means you'd get some exercise every day, and it's cheaper than gym membership. This would save money that could be spent on the dog's food and vet bills. You see? It all evens out. Also, everyone else has a pet and I've wanted a pet dog for so long, and I feel left out. And there are so many dogs out there that just need a good home... like ours? Love Darren

7) A balanced argument

8)

- a) Dr Helen Tenning concluded that "prolonged periods spent in front of a monitor can cause the eyes to glaze over permanently."
  b) "People who eat fewer than five pieces of fruit or vegetables each day tend to suffer from poor health," said Brian Fortescue, head of the government's healthy eating advisory committee.
  c) Professor McCoy of the Department of Confectionary-Related Risks at Tadley University agrees with the report — "Last month alone, more than seventeen students sustained irreparable damage to their clothes and schoolbooks because of failure to dispose of used gum in a proper manner."

9)

- Knitting is the fastest growing extreme sport in the UK. Popular with nans nationwide, knitting requires nimble fingers, fast reaction speeds and a good eye for colour. Knitting involves twisting wool into a series of knots by weaving it around pointy sticks, called needles, to make jumpers, cardigans and scarves. The most important skill is to learn to switch between knit and purl, the two stitches that make up most basic jumpers.

10) b) is less interesting because there is no varied use of language or detail, and there is no attempt to build up any suspense.

11)

- b) Can you believe that Mikey was spotted on a date with Laura?
  c) Why can't people be quiet when they're in the library?

Page 44 — Foundation Exam Questions

1) *A good answer should:*
- be in the format of a letter
- use informal language like "you" and "my" as the letter is to a friend
- use descriptive language so that your friend can imagine the birthday you had
- be clearly structured so that your friend understands the order of events
- use the five senses to make the writing more vivid/real

  Some points you could include in your answer:
- details of the birthday party (e.g. what you did, where you did it)
- why it was memorable (e.g. your Dad dropped the birthday cake)
- whether you expected it to be memorable (e.g. you had planned an enormous party in Ibiza), or dull (e.g. you had made no plans and all your friends were busy)
- your reaction to the events of the day and what you drew from the experience, e.g. positive or negative feelings

2) *A good answer should:*
- use language appropriate for talking to students at your school
- use informative language to make it clear where you did your work experience and what the order of events was
- use descriptive language and tell stories about what happened to make your explanation more interesting
- remember that an assembly is a formal situation

  Some points you could include in your answer:
- details of the work experience, e.g. how long you worked there, position held, location
- why you chose this particular company for your work experience
- how you set about getting in touch with the company to arrange your work experience, e.g. you wrote a letter
- how you felt before the first day, e.g. nervous or excited
- what your first impressions were and whether your colleagues were welcoming
- what the main challenges you faced during the work experience were, and how you overcame them
- what you drew from the experience, including positive or negative feelings

3) *A good answer should:*
- be written as if you're talking to teenagers
- use language suitable for a school newspaper

- explain why the charity needs their help and why this would be a good way to show their support
- give some quotes and facts to back up your argument — remember that you can make these up

  Some points you could include in your answer:
- any perks e.g. goody bag at the end of the walk provided by sponsors, a T-shirt with the charity's logo on it and a day off school
- it would look great on their CV
- the walk would also provide a physical challenge, sense of achievement and would provide an opportunity to make new friends
- reasons why physical fitness is important, e.g. prevention of heart disease and weight loss
- which charity you are doing the sponsored walk for and why it is a worthy cause
- what the fund-raising target is for the group and what impact this money could have
- that the target could be reached more easily if more students joined the walk and got sponsorship
- details about the walk, e.g. distance, difficulty, and dates of event

4) *A good answer should:*
- be in the format of a letter, e.g. it could have an opening paragraph explaining why you are writing
- be respectful and formal as the letter is from a pupil to their school governors
- put across your view about the concept of free musical instrument lessons for all pupils
- persuade the governors to adopt your point of view by using persuasive language e.g. personal stories

  Some points you could include in your answer:
- facts and statistics about the cost of providing free musical instrument lessons per pupil — remember you can make this up as long as it sounds reasonable
- whether most children would be likely to take advantage of the offer or not — if you want people to take you seriously, you could say you have done a survey to find this out
- your view about whether this would be a good use of school funds (e.g. a good use because of the benefits to students, such as increased confidence, or a waste of money and a distraction from studies)
- how you think learning a musical instrument compares to other possible activities at school, such as playing sport or taking part in a drama club, either positively or negatively
- what you feel the reaction of parents and students would be to your proposal

Page 46 — Higher Exam Questions

1)

- Start your letter in an appropriate way, e.g. "Dear Laura, I've just got back from the most amazing holiday, and I just had to write and tell you about it!"

- Come up with an interesting place, event or experience to write about. For example, "The highlight of the trip was a boat ride to the Whitsunday Islands on an inflatable power boat! We whooped, screamed and clung on for dear life as our fearless driver spun the boat in gravity-defying circles."

- Don't forget to include lots of descriptive techniques like similes, metaphors and personification. For example, "The iron grey waves growled and foamed menacingly under a leaden sky. My legs trembled and my stomach fluttered as though it was full of trapped hummingbirds, as I steeled myself to plunge in."

- Remember to vary your sentence structures and use some interesting punctuation. For example, "But oh, the difference once I opened my eyes! An underwater city greeted me, thronging with life: turrets and battlements of pink, green, grey coral, clown fish bustling busily, a leatherback turtle gliding by, intent on his private business. You would have loved it!"

- End your letter in a suitable way. For example, you might finish with something like: "Anyway, enough about me. I can't wait to hear all about your summer and I'm really looking forward to catching up when you get back from France. Lots of love, Eva".

2)

- You're writing a talk, so your introduction has to be appropriate for the purpose and for your audience. In this case you're not given a specific audience, so you need to assume that it's for adults, and write in a fairly formal style. For example: "Good evening Ladies and Gentlemen, and thank you for giving me the opportunity to come here tonight and talk to you about the work that my charity, Cakes For Kids, does here in the UK and further afield."

- You need to make sure that you cover both parts of the question — explaining what your charity does and informing the audience about how they can help. The clearest structure is to deal with one part, then move on to the second. Your first paragraph could start something like this: "I'd like to start tonight by explaining a little bit about what Cakes For Kids does, and why it's so important. Cakes for Kids started back in 1988, when I overheard a young girl on the bus explaining to her friend that, as well as going to school and doing her homework, she was also responsible for looking after her two younger siblings and helping her disabled mother to run the house. On the verge of tears, she said that things would be bearable, if only she felt that, just occasionally, someone was thinking of her, looking after her, letting her be a child."

- Once you've explained what your charity does, you need to deal with how the audience can help. The question asks you to inform, not persuade, so you need to give lots of information, but throwing in a few persuasive techniques certainly won't hurt. The second part of your answer could start like this: "I'm sure that by now you're all itching to get involved, to make life a bit more fun for these young people who are missing out on so much that most children take for granted. One of the main things we need is, of course, money. Buying baking ingredients and equipment and hiring venues doesn't come cheap. A donation of £10 will transport a child from their home to a country house, and provide the ingredients that will allow them to cover themselves in chocolate, throw flour at one another and produce something delicious to eat, all in the knowledge that, for once, they don't have to clean up afterwards. We also need volunteers..."

- You need to round off your talk in a suitable way, remembering who your audience is. For example: "Let me finish by, once again, thanking you for your time and attention. I hope I've given you a taste (no pun intended) of what Cakes For Kids hopes to achieve, and how you can help. If you'd like any more information, or if you'd like to get involved, I have some leaflets here for you to take home."

3)

- You're writing for a teen magazine, so making it clear that you're a teenager too will get your audience on your side. For example: "Like many teenagers, I have a pretty good grasp of what is going on in the world around me. I watch the news on TV, read newspapers and keep up to date with the internet. Yet the voting laws of this country mean we're treated as if we have all the understanding of a toddler."

- Once you've written a general introduction, launch into the main points of your argument. Remember to use techniques such as rhetorical questions and repetition. For example: "As a 16-year-old, I can legally get a full time job and be charged income tax, but I can't vote for who spends that tax money. I can join the army, but I can't vote for who says when we go to war. I can get married and start a family, but I can't make decisions about the country my kids will grow up in. Does any of this seem fair to you?"

- If you can come up with any counter-arguments, then include them, but make sure that you also explain why they don't ruin your case. For example: "Some people think that 16-year-olds aren't mature enough to have a say on serious political issues. But if we haven't been taught to think seriously about politics then maybe that's the fault of our schools, and that's something that might get fixed if we changed the minimum voting age. Besides, I know plenty of 16-year-olds who do think seriously about and care passionately about these issues, whereas there are millions of people in Britain aged over 18 who don't even care enough to vote."

- You could save your strongest point until last, because you know it will stick in your reader's mind. For example: "Many 16-year-olds care passionately about political issues, such as war and the environment. Some of these issues require urgent action and, since it's young people who'll live to see the worst effects of threats like global warming, surely young people should have a say in the government that's elected to tackle them. Maybe the thought of something bad happening in several decades is easier to put to the back of your mind if you know you probably won't be around then, but we will, and so we should be given the chance to bring about changes."

Page 56 — Warm-Up Questions

1) a) correct punctuation.
   c) paragraphs properly divided up.
   d) spelling all right.
2) Standard English is formal English that doesn't include any text speak, slang or dialect words.
3) You definitely need to use Standard English in your GCSE exam.
4)
- If you were writing a non-fiction text with direct speech it would be OK to put the speech in non-standard English — so long as that suited the person speaking.
5) a) Give me those pens.
   b) A barrister is a lawyer who speaks in court.
   c) The boy did as the teacher said.
6) Always start a sentence with a capital letter.
7) A full stop, a question mark or an exclamation mark.
8) Separating the parts of a list, to break up a long sentence to make it clearer and to add extra information in the middle of a sentence.
9) a) The man, who still hadn't recovered from his cold, was feeling ill.
   b) I need to buy chicken, cherries, chocolate, cheese and chips.
   c) Why won't Robert's dog play with the children's dog?
   d) Sarah asked, "Has anyone seen Liz today?"
   e) "Does anyone want another cup of tea?" Andy asked, "because I'm having one."
10) a) Charlie's dogs were eating bananas.
    b) I don't like Frank's new trousers.
    c) Mum says it's going to rain today.
11) This means, "I want to do an English exam."

Page 63 — Warm-Up Questions

1) a) affect
   b) there
   c) where
2) a) noun = horses, carriages
      verb = pulled
      adjective = enormous, heavy
      adverb = easily
   b) noun = Sonia, truth
      verb = wanted, know
      adjective = whole
      adverb = desperately
   c) noun = boys, headteacher, office
      verb = waited
      adjective = naughty, little
      adverb = nervously
3)
- a) The police car suddenly came to a stop near the abandoned wharf. The sirens continued to sound loudly.
- b) Scruffy pulled hard at the fraying lead, keen to get to the big river.
- c) The room was eerily silent. Jen looked around nervously. There were glinting shards of glass on the damp floor.
4) The subject is plural but the verb is singular. It should say "The children only eat sausages."
5) a) When I got home, I turned the television on.
   b) Today, I am happy.
6) a) When I get home, I will turn the television on.
   b) Tomorrow, I will be happy.
7) We began with a dish of lobster. The next course, beef, was well roasted and tender. The crème brulée was the perfect end to a delicious meal. I left completely satisfied.
8) —est
9) Katy's essay is much better than Claire's.
10) A simile says something is like something else. A metaphor says something is something else.
    • Simile: e.g. Revising for GCSEs is like walking down an endless gravel road, barefoot, under a blazing sun.
    • Metaphor: e.g. When you walk out of your last GCSE exam, you'll be in paradise.
11) a) Simile
    b) Metaphor
    c) Metaphor
    d) Simile
12) E.g. terrible, awful, dreadful.
13) a) I go rollerblading occasionally.
    b) Evacuate the building immediately!
    c) Fruit and vegetables are extremely nutritious.

Practice Exam — Foundation: Section A

1 a)

This question is testing your ability to select appropriate information from a text. So only write about the wand, and only write about stuff you can find out from the article.

You will be given one mark for each of the following points, up to a total of 4 marks:

- The Kymera wand can control televisions, computers, light switches and many other electrical household appliances.
- The Kymera wand is a remote control without any buttons.
- Chris Barnardo and Richard Blakesley are the inventors of the wand.
- The wand can control up to 13 different appliances.
- The wand responds to different movements and gestures, which is how it activates different appliances.
- The wand uses technology similar to the Nintendo Wii.
- The wand costs £49.95.
- The wand allows you to change volume by rotating the wand, or change channel by flicking your wrist.
- The wand runs on two AAA batteries.
- The wand changes to a low-power "sleep mode" after 60 seconds of inactivity.
- It has a three-axis accelerometer, which is how it tells when it is being moved.
- A piece of silicon detects which way up the wand is.
- The wand went on sale in September 2009.
- At the time the article was published, over 20,000 wands had been sold.
- At the time the article was published, the wand was being sold in 41 countries.

1 b)

This question is your chance to show that you've understood the article — read it carefully and only give answers that are relevant to the question. You could also back up your answers with quotes.

You will be given one mark for each point you make about Duncan Bannatyne's involvement, up to a total of four marks. Your responses may include:

- Duncan Bannatyne has invested £200,000 in the wand.
- Duncan Bannatyne was asked to invest by the inventors of the wand because he is a judge on Dragons' Den.
- Duncan Bannatyne now owns 20% of the business, in return for his investment.
- The inventors look forward to Duncan Bannatyne being involved "because of his vast business experience".
- The inventors expect Duncan Bannatyne's help will increase next year's turnover to £2 million.

- Duncan Bannatyne is enthusiastic about the project and thinks it will "do very, very well".

2)

This question asks you about two things — Jamie Oliver as a successful chef and Jamie Oliver as someone who helps people and animals. Make sure you make the same number of points for each part, and back up your answers with quotes. You will get one mark for each of the following reasons, up to eight marks:

Reasons for saying that Jamie Oliver is a successful chef:

- He has worked at "several prestigious restaurants" in England and Europe.
- He was a sous-chef at the Riverside Café.
- He is described as having "stormed onto the TV cooking scene".
- People loved his "simple, fun food".
- He was asked by Tony Blair to cook for the Italian prime minister.
- Tony Blair offered him a job as "food tsar".
- He opened his own chain of restaurants, which can be found "across the world".

Reasons for saying that Jamie Oliver helps people and animals:

- On his TV show *Jamie's Kitchen*, he taught "fifteen disadvantaged youngsters" to become chefs.
- He campaigned to get healthier food for school dinners.
- As a result of Jamie Oliver's campaign to improve school dinners, the government pledged to spend £280 million on them over 3 years.
- He made a TV programme about the suffering of battery-farmed chickens, which caused "massive increases" in sales of free-range and organic chickens.

3)

This question is different from the ones above — instead of finding information from the article, you should focus on the language. Look at how it is used to inform and advise the readers.

Here are some points you could make about the extract — you'll get up to 12 marks for this question:

Language used to inform:

- When the article is informing the reader, the writer sounds confident, for example, "some types of behaviour will be universally badly received". This kind of language tells the reader that the writer knows about the subject matter.
- Within the main article, there are several lists of examples which inform the reader. Lists of examples back up the information given and make it seem believable. By telling us that in China tourists hear "cries of 'Longwai!'; in East Africa the cry is 'Mzungu' and in Thailand 'Farang'" the author confirms his point about "surprising behaviour".

- The language in the fact box is descriptive, for example the "many toasts and a headache in the morning" found in Russia and Central Asia, or men who "hurl themselves off a platform with vines tied around their ankles" in Vanuatu. These details make the facts vivid, to inform the reader about the customs of these places.

Language used to advise:

- When offering advice, the article uses phrases such as "the best strategy" and "the best way". These phrases make the advice sound like friendly suggestions.

- The reader is told "you can get a handle on what to expect by reading guidebooks". The phrase "get a handle on" is informal, so it sounds more like a friend's advice than a strict order.

- The writer also uses "you" and "us" throughout the article so it seems that the advice is aimed directly at the reader.

4)

This question asks you to choose two of the three items and compare them. This means you have to say how they're similar and how they're different. Two aspects are mentioned — the layout of the text and use of pictures. Don't forget to discuss both in your answer.

You'll get a mark for each point up to 12 marks. Here are some points you could write about:

The layout of the text:

Dragons' Den

- It's a newspaper article, so it has a large, bold title.

- The title is also quite long — it gives a brief summary of the whole article, which means readers can tell at a glance what it is about.

- The paragraphs are very small and there is usually only one sentence in each paragraph. This means the article is broken up into easy-to-read chunks.

- The text is in columns so it is easy to read and clear.

Jamie Oliver

- It has a short title with just his name and no other information. This informs the reader about the subject of the article.

- A short summary of the article is given in big font in the middle of the text. This breaks up the block of text so it looks more appealing to readers. The summary gives the reader an idea of what the article is about, encouraging them to read on.

Local Customs

- It has a short title so you have to read more to find out exactly what the article is about.

- It's split into large paragraphs. Each paragraph gives an example of a problem and a solution, so there's a lot of information grouped together. This gives the impression that it is informative.

- The fact box is separated from the rest of the text and uses a coloured background. This is used to give extra information that's interesting to the reader. The fact box uses bullet points for the list of five entertaining examples. This makes them extremely easy to read.

The use of pictures:

Dragons' Den

- The photo's purpose is informative — it shows what the wand and its inventor looks like. It adds to the summary of the wand in the introduction.

- The photo makes the newspaper article look more interesting and colourful.

Jamie Oliver

- The photo's purpose is to show who Jamie Oliver is, so the reader knows who the profile is about.

- It is placed right at the beginning to back up the title.

Local Customs

- The photo is large and colourful, but it doesn't have a caption or relate to a particular point in the article. However, it shows a woman in traditional dress so it links to the general theme of the article which is local customs. This makes the reader think they might learn about some interesting local customs.

- Its purpose is both to make the article look interesting, so it is eye-catching, and to break up the text so the block of information looks more accessible.

Remember to compare the texts all the way through your answer and give reasons for your answers. For example, the newspaper article is laid out in small chunks that are quick to read and understand. This is because a newspaper appeals to people browsing and skim-reading. On the other hand, the Local Customs extract is aimed at people who are already interested in the subject of travel, so the text is large and more detailed.

Practice Exam — Foundation: Section B

5)

This question is an opportunity to be as imaginative as you want and to show off your descriptive language skills. The question is also testing your ability to 'explain', so make sure you explain why you like the celebrity in a clear and interesting way.

A good answer should:

- be in the format of a letter — i.e. start with "dear" or "to" and end with "love from" or "sincerely"

- use informal language like "you" and "my", as the letter is to a friend

- use a variety of interesting descriptive language techniques to describe your celebrity e.g. imagery

Some points you could include in your answer:

- why you've chosen to write about this celebrity — e.g. you've just read an interesting article about them.

- your opinion about the celebrity — whether you admire them, would like their job, or think they're fashionable.

- some viewpoints about the celebrity that are different from yours, and why you disagree with them.

- some techniques that could be included when explaining — a quote from the celebrity, statistics (e.g. percentage of people who admire him/her) etc.

6)

This is a 'persuade' question, so remember to keep your audience in mind. Feel free to make up some statistics to prove that your suggestions would improve road safety.

A good answer should:

- have the right form for a speech, e.g start by saying "Good morning Ladies and Gentleman"

- be respectful and formal as the speech is to the local council

- put across your view about the safety of the road at the moment

- persuade the council to improve the road by using techniques of persuasive language e.g. personal stories, rhetorical questions, lists, examples, quotations, examples of surveys, statistics

Some points you could include in your answer:

- The road doesn't have any traffic lights or zebra crossings to slow down traffic.

- The speed limit should be 20 mph, not 30 mph.

- There's no cycle path, so students have to cycle in the road.

- In addition to a safe crossing and cycle path, the pavements near to the school need to be widened. Children are more likely to walk or cycle to school, which is healthier and better for the environment.

- It is important that students feel the community respects them and is concerned for their safety.

- Drivers should set a good example, as many of the teenagers will soon be driving themselves.

Practice Exam — Higher: Section A

1)

- We learn that Piers Sellers is going to be "the last Briton to fly on a space shuttle". He is going to travel to the International Space Station and back again, a journey of 4.9 million miles. Sellers plans to take a piece of wood from the apple tree that inspired Sir Isaac Newton to come up with the theory of gravitation. The idea to take the wood is described as "a fun thing", and Sellers jokes about Isaac Newton being "spacesick", which shows that taking the wood is a light-hearted way of increasing public awareness of Newton's discoveries.

- Sellers intends to demonstrate Newton's laws — he says "it would have proved his first law of motion to be correct". This illustrates his respect for Isaac Newton, although his joke about how it would "confuse Isaac" suggests that he doesn't take his idea entirely seriously. This shows that the text has been written to entertain, as well as inform.

- Keith Moore, the head librarian at the Royal Society, backs up the idea that the mission is intended to capture the public's imagination by saying the "idea is that this will inspire people. You can begin to talk to schoolchildren about science". This suggests that part of the reason for Sellers taking the piece of tree is to encourage young people to engage with science, and to show that it can be fun and interesting.

- Sellers is also undertaking the mission to help the Royal Society celebrate their 350th anniversary. The article tells us that Sellers approached the Royal Society to ask to "take something up" into space. This suggests that he wants the Society to be involved in the mission, possibly because Isaac Newton was once president of it.

2)

- The page heading "Be Inspired" is in a dark blue box, which makes it stand out from the rest of the text. By highlighting the word "spire" using italics and a white font, the title links to the image next to it, which shows some of Oxford's spires at sunset. The photo has a sepia tone, which gives it a dreamy, historic feeling, and reinforces the text's message that Oxford is a "hive of history".

- There is another photograph and a video on the page, both of which show ancient buildings under a bright blue sky. This makes Oxford look warm and inviting, and shows that it has beautiful buildings. This supports the primary purpose of the text, which is to persuade people to visit the city.

- Both photos show green, open space, which makes them look like pleasant places to visit and backs up the text box that talks about "Open spaces in the city". The image of New College acts as a virtual tour; the age and architecture of the building make you wonder what it's like inside, which persuades you to watch it. By watching the virtual tour, people will find out more about the city, which will make them want to see it for themselves. The captions mention different things that visitors can do in Oxford, so they are also persuasive.

- The blue colour in the photographs is echoed in the rest of the text; the left-hand menu, text boxes and subheadings are all in blue. Blue is a calming colour, so it makes the reader feel relaxed and backs up the text, which describes Oxford as having "plenty of room to relax".

- The text is broken up using subheadings and text boxes. This makes it easier to take in the information, so it supports one of the purposes of the text, which is to inform readers about what Oxford is like and what there is to do there. The two text boxes contrast "A modern metropolis" with the "Open spaces in the city", ensuring that the text appeals to a wide range of readers. The menu on the left-hand side of the page makes it clear where people can go to get more information. As well as making the text more informative, this also makes it more persuasive, because it shows how easy it is for people to research their trip.

3)

- In the first paragraph, the narrator describes himself as "Hunched" and "a zombie father", which suggest that he views himself as a monster who will frighten his own children. He says that his son treated him like "an unpredictable animal", reinforcing the feeling that he is worried about frightening or hurting his children. However, his son's movements are "tender", and he says that his daughter "covers my forehead with noisy kisses", showing the narrator's relief and gratitude that they still love him.

- The narrator says that he is "a shadow, a tiny fragment of a dad", which suggests that he feels inadequate and wishes that he could be a complete father to his children. However, he acknowledges that he is "still a dad", showing his realisation that you never leave the ties of parenthood behind, and his determination that he will still be the best parent he can be to his children.

- He says that he is "torn between joy" at being with his family and "fear" that seeing him is not the "ideal entertainment" for his children. This shows how happy he is to see them, and also how unselfish his love is; he sees them because it is best for them, not just for him.

- He describes the "Beach Club" as a "neutral zone" between the hospital and the outside world, giving the impression that he regards the two as enemies who are at war, or at least too far removed from one another to ever really overlap. This highlights his fear, and his feeling of isolation from the rest of the world. To overcome this fear, he imagines his wheelchair as a "chariot", implying that he wishes he was a hero, rather than an invalid.

- It is clear that the narrator feels the loss of speech very keenly; he says "my communication system disqualifies repartee", showing that he wishes he could make a witty comment and communicate normally with his children. Instead he feels boring, describing his "forced lack of humour" as one of the worst things about his situation.

- In the final paragraph, the narrator's main feeling is sorrow. He misses physical contact with his son, the "simple right to ruffle his bristly hair". He returns to his earlier worries about being "monstrous", and frightening his children, silently appealing to his son "Don't be scared". He creates a link between himself and his son's drawing of the "condemned man", showing that he feels trapped by his illness; the mention of "the gallows" give the impression that he is also waiting for death.

4)

- The purpose of Item 2 is to inform and persuade. It mentions lots of locations in Oxford, for example Port Meadow and the Botanic Garden, which give the reader the impression that the writer knows Oxford well and is knowledgeable about it. This makes the reader trust the writer, which makes them more likely to pay attention to the text. In contrast, Item 3 aims to entertain, so it doesn't refer to facts and specific details, but instead describes the narrator's feelings. For example, he says "I will never tire of seeing them walk alongside me". Describing what he is experiencing makes the reader empathise with the writer, which helps them to relate to the text and understand what he is going through.

- Item 2 is written in the third person, for example "the jewel in the crown of this historic city is its university", which makes it seem more authoritative. This supports one of the purposes of the text, which is to inform. However, the writer also addresses the reader directly, for example "if you can drag yourself from the comfort of one of Oxford's superb hotels", which helps the reader to engage with the text and therefore makes it more persuasive. It also makes the tone of the article seem more chatty, as though a friend is informing you about what you can do in the city. Item 3 is written in the first person, for example "I have become something of a zombie father". This makes it clear to the reader that the narrator is describing something that really happened to him, which makes his sadness seem more personal. This makes the reader want to find out what happened next, because they feel connected to the writer.

- Item 2 uses metaphors like "the jewel in the crown", which makes the university sound precious and celebrated, and lots of superlatives, such as "most celebrated minds" and "oldest", which show that it is one of the best and most established universities. Positive language such as this reinforces the message that Oxford is a great place to visit. Item 3 also uses vivid imagery, in this case to create a contrast between the "energetic and noisy" children and the father who is a "tiny fragment of a dad". The narrator describes himself as "a rough sketch, a shadow", which makes the reader understand how incomplete and insignificant he feels, so that we can empathise with his condition. He uses a metaphor to describe his loss of conversational skill, "the keenest rapier grows dull".

This makes the reader understand how precious simple things like conversation are, and therefore reinforces the text's message, that it is important to live life to the full while you can.

- Item 2 uses rhetorical questions such as "what better way to round off your visit than by looking down over the city from one of its tallest towers?", which challenge the reader and make them feel that they have no reason not to do as the writer suggests. Alliteration such as "hive of history" and "cheap chance" makes the text seem friendly and fun, which makes the reader feel that they will enjoy visiting the city. The writer of Item 3 varies his sentence length to emphasise his feelings and reinforce important points. Most of the sentences are quite long and complex, making them flow and giving them a slow, sad feeling which emphasises the narrator's sorrow. He switches to shorter sentences when he is overwhelmed by sorrow: "Grief surges over me.", "Suddenly, I can take no more." This makes it sound as though he is too upset to form longer sentences, and also highlights these emotions, making them seem particularly raw and therefore encouraging the reader to engage with the narrator.

Practice Exam — Higher: Section B

5)

- Dear....,

    You must be sick of hearing me chatter on about my sister's baby daughter, Katie (I think I babble more than my niece does!). But I'm convinced that if you meet her you'll love her just as much as I do, and I'd like a fellow member in the cult of Katie! It will also provide an ideal opportunity for you to see for yourself whether or not she's got the family nose (I fear she has, poor mite). I've got to take some of Mum's old baby stuff over there on Saturday, so I wondered if you'd like to come with me. What do you think?

    My sister is really looking forward to catching up with you, and said to remind you of your promise to baby sit when Tim takes her out for her birthday meal next month. Saturday could be a good opportunity for you and Katie to get to know one another, so she (and indeed you) won't howl all night when left alone! We'll also need your prodigious appetite, as Helen's nesting instinct went into overdrive and she's stocked up on enough biscuits and frozen pizzas to last until Katie's grown up and left home. I wanted to tell her that she's just looking after a baby, not preparing for a nuclear winter, but I thought it might be a bit cruel...

    Anyway, I'm so excited for you to meet my little niece. When she laughs I just get bowled over by a wave of nostalgia — it takes me right back to when your brother was a baby. Of course, he's concrete evidence that she won't be a baby for long, so come on down before she turns into a stroppy teenager....

6)

- Of course you could argue that the lives of boy band members and WAGs have no place in the public consciousness. You could even argue that the media has an ethical duty not to give these people status that they don't deserve and inevitably can't handle. But that is no reason to become stuck up or snobbish about people whose only claim to fame is being famous.

    For a start, these dazzling reality show stars provide an important service for modest civilians whose lives would be the poorer without the occasional indulgent wallow in some C-list dirt. It might seem like a big claim, but I would argue that followers of celebrities find their lives enriched by their involvement in the lives of others. Having public figures who people can collectively discuss, adore and despise, serves to unite vast swathes of the population. What's more, on a serious note, public and media responses to the actions of famous people can teach important moral lessons and highlight the implications of certain behaviour: generosity or infidelity, for example.

    "Sounds like gossip," I hear you say. Well, you may be right, but then gossip can be the beginning of an interest in other people and the trials and tribulations they face. Cultivated and nurtured, a healthy interest in other people's dirty laundry can have a positive effect on your own life, because you can reassure yourself that at least you haven't got it as bad as them. And you certainly can't sniff at that.

Glossary

audience	The people who will <u>read</u> a piece of writing.
caption	A line of text under a photograph or picture, telling you <u>what it shows</u>.
dialect	The different words or sentence constructions that are used by people from a specific place, e.g. the non-standard grammar in "I <u>were</u> running away".
emotive language	Language that has an <u>emotional</u> effect on the reader, e.g. the phrase "horrific scenes of destruction" will make the reader feel angry and disgusted.
exaggeration	Describing something as <u>more</u> than it really is. E.g. "She was a million miles from home".
form	The <u>type</u> of text, e.g. a letter, a speech or a magazine article.
headline	The statement at the <u>top</u> of a text (e.g. a newspaper article), usually in a <u>large font</u>, used to attract readers' interest by giving an impression of what it's about.
language	The <u>choice of words</u> used. The language affects how the piece of writing will influence the reader, e.g. it can be persuasive.
layout	The way a piece of writing is <u>presented</u> to the reader. E.g. what kind of <u>font</u> is used, whether there are subheadings, the use of photographs, whether text columns are used.
list of three	Using <u>three</u> adjectives together to make an argument or description sound more effective. E.g. "It was a cold, dark and stormy night."
metaphor	A way of describing something by saying that it <u>is something else</u>, to create a vivid image. E.g. "His eyes were deep, black, oily pools."
non-fiction	Writing about the <u>real world</u>, rather than making up a story.
purpose	The <u>reason</u> someone writes a text. E.g. to persuade, to argue, to advise.
quotation	Exactly what someone said, which is added to a piece of writing using speec E.g. the Prime Minister said, "there's no problem", about the crisis.
rhetorical question	A question which <u>doesn't need an answer</u> and tries to persuade the reader to agree with the writer. E.g. "Are we really expected to put up with this government's lies?"
simile	A way of describing something by <u>comparing</u> it to something else, usually by using the word "like" or "as". E.g. "He was as pale as the moon."
slang	Words or phrases that sound <u>informal</u> or <u>conversational</u>, e.g. "bloke", "telly".
statistics	<u>Figures</u> from research, which are added to a piece of writing to <u>back up</u> points. E.g. "80% of parents agree that school uniform is too expensive."
structure	The <u>order</u> and <u>arrangement</u> of a piece of writing. E.g. how the text begins, develops and ends, whether it uses subheadings or not.
style	The <u>way</u> a text is <u>written</u>, e.g. the type of language and techniques used.
subheading	A word or phrase that <u>stands out</u> from the text and <u>divides</u> the text into chunks. It gives an idea of what the <u>next section</u> of text is about.
tenses	Writing about the <u>past</u>, <u>present</u> or <u>future</u>. E.g. "I walked" is the past tense, "I walk" is the present tense and "I will walk" is the future tense.
tone	The <u>mood</u> of a piece of writing, e.g. happy, sad, serious, lighthearted.
vocabulary	The range of <u>words</u> used.

Index

E12S41